75E   935

ESSAYS in the HISTORY of NEW YORK CITY

Kennikat Press
National University Publications
Interdisciplinary Urban Series

ESSAYS IN THE HISTORY OF NEW YORK CITY:

A MEMORIAL TO SIDNEY POMERANTZ

edited by

IRWIN YELLOWITZ

National University Publications
KENNIKAT PRESS // 1978
Port Washington, N. Y. // London

Manufactured in the United States of America

Published by
Kennikat Press Corp.
Port Washington, N.Y./London

Library of Congress Cataloging in Publication Data
Main entry under title:

Essays in the history of New York City.

(Interdisciplinary urban series) (National university publications)
Bibliography: p.
Includes index.
CONTENTS: Wisan, J. E. Sidney Pomerantz, scholar and teacher.—Still, B. New York's mayors.—Pessen, E. Political democracy and the distribution of power in antebellum New York City. [etc.]
1. New York (City)—History—1775–1865—Addresses, essays, lectures. 2. New York (City)—History—1865–1898—Addresses, essays, lectures. 3. Pomerantz, Sidney Irving, 1909- —Addresses, essays, lectures. I. Pomerantz, Sidney Irving, 1909-   II. Yellowitz, Irwin.
F128.44.E87   974.7'1'04   77-21758
ISBN 0-8046-9208-4

CONTENTS

FROM THE PUBLISHER

If those who came to pay their last respects to Sidney Pomerantz had been garbed in their caps and gowns the gathering might have been mistaken for a convocation of some of the finest intellects of New York.

At the conclusion of the memorial service I approached Dr. Irwin Yellowitz, one of our distinguished authors, and asked if he would like to serve as editor of a commemorative tribute to Sidney. Without hesitation he agreed. Much time and effort went into the selection of the contributors who represent a fine cross-section of Sidney Pomerantz's colleagues at CUNY, fellow historians, former students now highly esteemed in their own right—all of whom contributed their essays for no recompense and who waived all royalties. Those royalties with a matching contribution from the publisher will be donated to the City College Fund as a fitting tribute to one to whom City College meant so very much.

Accompanying the manuscript was a letter from Dr. Yellowitz with the following as the last paragraph:

I am personally very happy to send you this set of essays. Sidney was one of the finest persons that I have met in academic life. All those who contributed share my feelings for this fine and gentle man. Sidney's memory deserves to be honored, and I hope this volume will do him justice.

In echoing these sentiments, the publisher, also a City College alumnus, dedicates this book to the fond memory of an esteemed cousin, good friend, and ever available counselor.

ESSAYS in the HISTORY of NEW YORK CITY

CONTRIBUTORS

SELMA BERROL is Professor of History and Assistant Dean of Liberal Arts at the Baruch School, CUNY.

MARK D. HIRSCH is Professor Emeritus of History and former chairman of the department at Bronx Community College.

EDWARD PESSEN is Distinguished Professor of History at Baruch College and at the Graduate School and University Center, CUNY.

DONALD SIMON is Director of Development at the Brooklyn Center of Long Island University.

RICHARD SKOLNIK is an Associate Professor of History at the City College, CUNY.

BAYRD STILL is Professor Emeritus of History at New York University.

JOSEPH E. WISAN is Professor Emeritus of History of the City College, CUNY.

IRWIN YELLOWITZ is Professor of History at the City College, CUNY.

JOSEPH E. WISAN

SIDNEY POMERANTZ, SCHOLAR AND TEACHER

The City College of New York, and particularly its Department of History, played a major role in Sidney Pomerantz's life. It meant much to him, and he to it.

As an undergraduate at City College (class of 1930), he distinguished himself as a brilliant student. Sidney was close to the top of his class, was elected to Phi Beta Kappa, and won several medals and prizes. He was especially proud of winning the history department's own prize (later renamed the Nelson P. Mead prize) for the best performance on an oral examination. His professors regarded him as one of the best students of the decade.

Sidney Pomerantz distinguished himself, too, in the Columbia University Graduate School, earning his master's degree in 1932 and his doctorate in 1938. His doctoral dissertation, "New York: An American City, 1783-1803," was a pioneer work in urban history and an original contribution to an understanding of our nation's early years. When published it was most favorably reviewed in the major scholarly organs. When it was republished many years later (with a new foreword) it was again greeted most enthusiastically by eminent historians. It was, and still is, the definitive work on the period and a classic book in American urban history.

The qualities that characterized his dissertation—sound scholarship, intelligent analysis, and clear presentation—were to distinguish Sidney Pomerantz's writings throughout his career. His chapter "The Patriot Newspaper and the American Revolution" in *The Era of the American Revolution*, edited by Richard B. Morris, was a splendid article evoking

3

high praise from a host of knowledgeable critics, including Frank Luther Mott. Interestingly, this article was an outgrowth, in part, of an essay Sidney had prepared as an undergarduate. Another article, "Newspaper Humor in the War for Independence," was, in the words of Merle Curti, "an instructive and delightful piece." Of the centennial article, "The City of New York in the Year 1847," Allan Nevins wrote, "It is a really capital article, full of meat and touched with grace." These are typical of the very many expressions of appreciation Sidney's work received from leading scholars and critics.

Sidney Pomerantz was a prolific and eagerly sought book reviewer, particularly in the fields of American economic and business history, journalism, and the history of New York. His reviews appeared in a wide range of scholarly journals, including the *American Historical Review*, the *Annals* of the American Academy of Political and Social Science, the *American Political Science Review*, the *Journalism Quarterly*, and *New York History*, and they were characterized by sound judgment, vast learning, objectivity, and clarity of expression. In the scores of reviews from his pen, there is a complete absence of bias or nit-picking.

After several years of summer session teaching, Sidney joined the permanent staff of the City College of New York in 1941 as an instructor. He was promoted to the rank of assistant professor in 1949, associate professor in 1954, and professor in 1960. Promotions were slow in those days, and his chairman wrote in 1953, when recommending the associate rank, that "Professor Pomerantz is one of the ablest and most useful members of the History Department, regardless of rank." It should be recalled, too, that the history department at C.C.N.Y. was one of the best undergraduate departments in the country.

As a teacher, Sidney had no superior. Shy and retiring as he appeared in private contacts with his colleagues, the classroom seemed to transform him into an energetic, self-possessed, poised extrovert who gave of himself without stint or reservation. His thorough mastery of subject matter, richness of anecdote and illustrative material, keen insights into motives and movements, clarity of thought and expression, and occasional flights into eloquence enriched and enlivened his classes. His students, almost without exception, were grateful. One wrote, "I have never done anything like this before, but I felt I must tell you how much I enjoyed your class; I should say how much *we* enjoyed your class." Indeed many of Sidney's students were inspired to continue in history and related fields, and a goodly number of them now occupy important academic posts throughout the country.

Until his death, Sidney kept in touch with many of them, and he was intensely proud of their achievements.

His contributions to the Department of History, to City College, and later to the Graduate School of the City University of New York, were unique, continuous, and most substantial. Sidney Pomerantz had a wealth of experience in giving courses at all levels. He contributed substantially to the organization and modification of several required and intermediate courses at City College. He taught a number of elective courses in American history with great success, and he brought to his teaching a special interest in the use of audiovisual aids, field trips to museums and historical societies, and other devices to enrich instruction. While at the School of Business and Public Administration of City College, Sidney introduced a course titled "The History of American Business Enterprise" that won notice outside the institution (see *Bulletin* of the Business Historical Society, June, 1949). His graduate course, "The History of the City and State of New York," which he first offered in the School of Education, received wide recognition, and Sidney prepared an account of it for *American Heritage* (October, 1948). In addition, he developed a graduate seminar and colloquium, "The Nature and Problems of Metropolitan New York," a field in which he did extensive research, much of it unfortunately still unpublished at his death.

His role in the establishment and progress of graduate work in the history department at City College was pivotal. He served on key committees; he organized top-drawer conferences dealing with urban history and related fields; and he made a major contribution in securing the Rockefeller and Littauer Foundation grants for the New York Area program, which was introduced at City College in 1954. Sidney also served as Secretary of the New York Area Research Council, and during the New York Area Research Project, he supervised the work of the graduate assistants engaged in that field. At a later date, a number of the best doctoral dissertations prepared in the early years of the Graduate School of the City University of New York were completed with Sidney Pomerantz's guidance or under his direction.

Sidney's professional qualities were enhanced by his unique and charming personality. His outstanding traits were modesty, gentleness, intellectual and moral integrity, and complete dedication to his students and his profession. On occasion, Sidney would exhibit a wry sense of humor, usually unexpected and always delightful. He was conscientious to a fault. Frail in body, but robust in spirit, he rarely missed a class or an assignment.

His devotion to duty was so complete that at times he drove himself too hard, and he would shrug off suggestions that he relax. He seemed happiest and most at home in the classroom or the library. Sidney was extremely well read. He subscribed to scores of scholarly magazines, almost to hobby dimensions, and his conversations on most subjects revealed a wide and deep knowledge and understanding.

Sidney Pomerantz's colleagues respected and admired his intellectual ability and his achievements, and they loved him as a precious human being. The essays that follow are a tribute to this fine teacher and scholar from some of those who worked with him and knew him. All the essays treat topics in the history of New York City, which was his major lifelong interest. It is hoped that this volume continues the spirit of the accomplishments of Sidney Pomerantz.

BAYRD STILL

1

NEW YORK'S MAYORS:
THE INITIAL GENERATION

The mayoralty of New York is one of the most venerable institutions not only of the city but of the nation. The office has existed for more than three hundred years, which makes the presidency of the United States young by comparison. The mayoral office has grown in power and responsibility in this three-century span, reaching a peak of specified authority in the city charter that became effective on January 1, 1963. This charter strengthened the mayor's budgetary power and enhanced his potential for leadership by giving him broad authority to organize administrative agencies. His role in budget making was somewhat limited in a new charter that went into effect on January 1, 1977, a development prompted by the city's fiscal difficulties; but the mayor remains a powerful figure not only because of existing constituted authority but because of his role as the city's chief advocate at a time when the city's salvation depends upon the cooperation and good will both of organized local agencies and of the state and federal governments.

The contrast between the stated powers of today's mayor and those of his seventeenth-century predecessors, in the initial generation of the office, has created the impression that New York City's mayors were primarily figureheads. Closer examination reveals, however, that this was not so. In the initial generation of the office the mayors were invariably men of political and administrative capacity and experience, as well as economic achievement. They were selected because of their leadership role in the local society, and more often than not because their choice would strengthen the provincial government with the dominant Dutch element, or factions thereof, in the community. In their background of experience through prior participation in local government, their relationship to influential ethnic elements in the local society, and their active involvement in municipal administration, New York City's seventeenth-century mayors anticipated their successors of the present day.[1]

The mayoralty in New York is a heritage of British dominion in the New World. The English took possession of what is now New York City in 1664, when New Amsterdam, progenitor of the modern city, was less than forty years old and numbered fewer than two thousand inhabitants. The Dutch relinquished control on August 29, 1664, but the conversion of the municipal government from a Dutch to an English pattern did not occur until nearly ten months later. Then, on June 12, 1665, Governor Richard Nicolls revoked "the fforme and Ceremony of Government . . . under the name . . . of Sc[h]out, Burgomasters, & Schepens," the Dutch pattern of city administration, and substituted government by a "Mayor Aldermen & Sherriffe," the time-honored officialdom of British municipal government.[2]

The new officials were to be appointed by the British governor, as their predecessors had been by the Dutch director general. There were other similarities between the new municipal officialdom and that of Dutch days. The newly created mayor had duties somewhat similar to those of the schout, who under the Dutch had served as presiding officer, administrator, public prosecutor, and legislator, and whose responsibilities in the area of law enforcement had given him a role similar to that of the English sheriff. Aldermen replaced the Dutch burgomasters and schepens, but they exercised legislative and judicial functions similar to those of their Dutch counterparts.[3]

In one respect the new English pattern provided less representative government than that of New Amsterdam. Though the Dutch officials had not been elected, a measure of representative government had operated in their choice: the incumbent officials nominated their successors by presenting a double number of nominees from which the Dutch director general made his appointments. They could, indeed, nominate themselves for reappointment, but they were obliged to make alternate nominations as well. This quasi-representative practice, though no manifestation of really popular government, was traditional in the Netherlands; it continued to be exercised in New York after the British took over, until Nicolls reconstituted the municipal government along British lines. The loss of the right to nominate, under the new pattern of government, aggravated already existing tensions between the new British authority and the Dutch citizenry.[4]

Given the recency of the British conquest, it is understandable that New York City's first mayor was someone identified with British authority. It nevertheless is significant that Governor Nicolls selected a person for the position who gave promise of being acceptable to the Dutch as well. This was Thomas Willett, a New Englander who had been one of the British emissaries during the surrender negotiations but who had also had close relations with the Dutch community for a number of years before the British took over. Though British by birth, New York City's first mayor had lived in Leyden, in Holland, for a time prior to his migration to the Plymouth colony; presumably, he spoke Dutch; and although he held civil and military posts in the Plymouth settlement, he also owned property in New Netherland, traded out of New Amsterdam, and maintained friendly relations with the Dutch government there. On several occasions he had acted on its behalf in boundary disputes and negotiations with the Indians. Apparently he was on such good terms with Peter Stuyvesant that on the eve of the British conquest he warned the Dutch governor of Britain's plans and counseled capitulation. This identification with both conqueror and conquered made Willett an especially appropriate choice for mayor in the period of transition from Dutch to English rule, and it suggests that the British early recognized the importance of public acceptance of their appointees to the office of mayor.[5]

Men of English background held the office of mayor in the first three years after the British conquest. Willett served two separate terms, and in the intervening year the mayor was Thomas Delavall, a member of Nicolls's command at the time of the conquest. Then, in 1668, Governor Nicolls for the first time appointed a member of the local Dutch citizenry to the office. This was Cornelis Steenwyck, who, though historians have taken little note of his accomplishments, deserves recognition as one of New York City's memorable mayors. A native of Holland, Steenwyck had settled in New Amsterdam by 1651 and had quickly attained prominence as a merchant-trader, sending his vessels to Virginia and the West Indies and later engaging in European trade. He also had already played an active role in local government. He had held the office of schepen in 1658 and 1660, was chosen burgomaster in 1662, 1664, and 1665, and had served as one of the commissioners for the Dutch in the surrender negotiations of 1664. According to the report, he was by the time of his appointment as mayor not only the most popular man in New York, but also the best dressed—an estimation supported by a contemporary portrait owned by the New-York Historical Society. Yet even more impressive than the richness of the velvet jacket and broad lace collar are the sharp-featured directness and strength of personality which the portrait reveals.[6]

Whether community pressure or political instinct prompted Nicolls to choose Steenwyck the records do not make clear; but it was soon apparent that he was using his position to bring about changes beneficial to the Dutch residents. Toward the close of Steenwyck's first term as mayor, the magistrates regained the privilege of nominating their successors. This concession was made by the new governor, Francis Lovelace, who succeeded Nicolls in August 1668. Lovelace appeared to be desirous of gaining the support of the municipal corporation, in line with Britain's policy of encouraging the growth of American commercial centers. With the consent of the duke of York he offered to make any "reasonable and practicable" changes "for the better regulation" of the city that the mayor and aldermen should suggest. The only change they proposed was the return to the Dutch practice of choosing the magistrates from a double number of nominees, and this the governor respected in his choices in October 1669.

From 1669 to 1672 Lovelace chose the mayors as well as the aldermen from nominees presented by the incumbents, a practice that made the mayor representative of something more than the governor's will alone. Lovelace reappointed Steenwyck in 1669, but for the next three terms selected men of English background—Thomas Delavall, Matthias Nicolls, and John Lawrence. Nicolls, no relative of the former governor, was a lawyer with broad administrative experience in the province. Lawrence, a well-to-do merchant trader, though born in England, had lived in New Amsterdam before the British conquest and was much respected among the Dutch. Although the choice of men of English background may have been prompted by the growing tension between the Dutch and English abroad, the replacement of Steenwyck does not suggest that he was out of favor; Lovelace appointed him to his council in 1670, and when the governor went to Delaware in the spring of 1672, he left Steenwyck and Delavall in charge.[7]

International complications led to the temporary reconquest of New York by the Dutch in 1673, a development apparently welcomed by most of the residents. During the fifteen months of Dutch rule (from August 9, 1673, to November 10, 1674), the office of mayor was eliminated, and the management of local affairs was again vested in a schout, burgomasters, and schepens. Ex-mayor Steenwyck continued to be the spokesman for the community under the restored Dutch government, as he had been under English rule. He was given the post of counselor of New Netherland and was to assist the new governor in "all cases relative to justice and police," as well as to advise him on military matters. The Dutch even appointed him governor of Acadia, a newly acquired province, but this post he never assumed.[8]

With the restoration of British authority in 1674, the mayoralty was reinstituted, and the new British governor, Sir Edmund Andros, installed former mayor Matthias Nicolls in the office. Steenwyck remained for the time the leader of the opposition, and as such endeavored to ensure that the British would respect local rights. Tension was aggravated by the fact that the resumption of British control promised to curtail trade with the Netherlands—a matter of practical importance to the local leaders, virtually all of whom were merchant-traders. The Dutch also resented the authoritarian attitude of Governor Andros, who refused to confirm the earlier guarantees which absolved New Yorkers of Dutch background from having to fight against their former countrymen. When Andros demanded an oath of allegiance to England, the Dutch merchants, led by Steenwyck, refused to comply and even threatened to leave the province. Thereupon Andros accused Steenwyck and most of his associates of sedition, imprisoned them, and confiscated their property until they would agree to take the oath.[9]

Though the merchants finally gave in, their resistance and the threat of their possible migration from the province probably convinced Andros that he ought to accord more recognition in municipal office to representatives of the original residents. In the succeeding fifteen years most of New York City's mayors were of Dutch background. One of these was the city's first native-born mayor, Stephanus Van Cortlandt, the son of Oloff Stevenszen Van Cortlandt, one of the wealthiest and most prominent members of New York's early Dutch society, and a figure of consequence in his own right.[10]

In 1683 the citizenry gained the privilege of electing the aldermen, another achievement in which one can see ex-Mayor Cornelis Steenwyck's fine *"Nieuw Amsterdamische"* hand. For some years the local residents had been complaining about the lack of representative government in New York on both the provincial and local levels—increasingly so as the grant of self-government in neighboring Pennsylvania emphasized by contrast the lack of representative institutions in New York. In 1681, Steenwyck and John Lawrence, another former mayor, served on a grand jury that petitioned the duke of York for a representative assembly for the province. Shortly thereafter, the duke agreed to the request on the condition that such an assembly would raise a revenue for the province. Moreover, the duke, perhaps mindful of the wealth concentrated in the port of New York, professed his willingness to do something for the city as well. He instructed the new governor, Thomas Dongan, to consider, with the governor's council, the advisability of granting to New York City "immunities and priviledges" beyond what "other parts of my territoryes doe enjoy."[11]

Shortly after his arrival in New York the new governor solicited the views of the magistrates (the mayor and the aldermen) on the subject, and on November 9, 1683, they presented their requests. Chief of these was their desire for an elected, rather than an appointed, municipal council—a reform on the local level similar to what had been sought for the province at large. They proposed that the city be divided into six wards and that in each the freemen should elect, once every year, "their own officers"—not only an alderman for each ward but also a common councilman (a new position) and such minor officials as constables, overseers of the poor, scavengers, and the like, all of whom formerly had been appointed.[12]

It seems more than coincidence that at this juncture Cornelis Steenwyck was again in a position not only to advocate this reform but also to help ensure its realization. To begin with, although he was not an alderman at the time, his signature, along with that of Nicholas Bayard, another leading citizen of Dutch birth, appears on the magistrates' reply to Governor Dongan, in which they stated their request for an elected council, unmistakable evidence of Steenwyck's position of leadership in the community. Moreover, by the end of the month, on November 24, 1683, Dongan appointed Steenwyck as mayor (the new governor's first appointee to that office) and named Bayard one of the members of a completely reconstituted board of aldermen. What prompted these moves one can only conjecture, but there seems little doubt that Dongan, in selecting Steenwyck, thought it appropriate to vest the mayoralty in the most influential citizen of the community.[13]

The new municipal government, with Steenwyck at its head, now moved to ensure the realization of the November 9 proposals. They knew that these needed the sanction of the duke of York to become official; nevertheless, after only three days in office, Steenwyck and the aldermen asked that the proposals be put into practice pending the duke's approval.

As if to suggest that delay on the governor's part would give them time to think up new demands, they requested additional concessions that would have increased the number of elected officials beyond the number asked on November 9 and would have provided further privileges for the municipal corporation. Dongan's annoyance at the magistrates' impatience suggests that, for all his reputed liberality, he might have delayed implementing their requests had Steenwyck and the magistrates failed to press the case. Nevertheless, on December 10, 1683, Dongan conceded that the proposals made by the magistrates on November 9 for the "Weal and Government" of the city be "put in practice until such time as his Royall highness' pleasure shall be further known." It presumably is not without relevance that on the same day that the governor made these concessions a committee composed of Steenwyck, John Lawrence, William Beekman, and John Inians was making arrangements for the collection of what euphemistically was called a "free and voluntary present to the Governor." It also is pertinent to note the "mayoral experience" on this committee, represented not only in Steenwyck and Lawrence, but in Beekman, who as deputy mayor had been acting mayor from September 1681 to October 1683.[14]

The governor's concessions and their implementation in the course of the ensuing year established the practice of representative government for New York City two years before the principle was embodied in the Dongan charter of 1686. Nor did the mayor and aldermen allow the governor time to change his mind. On December 10, the very day of Dongan's concession, the magistracy took steps to institute the immediate election, by the "freeholders and freemen" in the several wards, of common councilmen, assessors, and constables. These elected officers, along with the incumbent aldermen, served until October 1684, when they were succeeded by newly elected officials, including the aldermen. Meanwhile, the creation of the office of recorder (another request of the November 9 petition) had been authorized. One may well wonder whether these gains would have been so speedily achieved without the initiative and leadership of the mayor, especially since the hoped-for representative government at the provincial level was delayed in realization.[15]

Developments in other areas exhibit the vigor and innovating spirit of Steenwyck's mayoral administration. Committees of the magistrates were appointed to look into the condition of the public revenue, to review the public works, and to provide information for codifying the city ordinances. The magistrates pressed the governor for permission to exploit new sources

of revenue in the form of dock fees and licenses, and they waged a successful campaign to get the governor to reconfirm for the city's inhabitants
the monopoly of grinding flour and producing bread and biscuit for export,
on which it was thought the economic welfare of the community depended.
The corporation proceeded vigorously against people who were in arrears
with tax payments and the payment of dockage fees, and they expanded
urban services by establishing a paid citizen watch to go the rounds nightly
under the supervision of the elected constables. The minutes of the common council for 1683 and 1684 convey the impression that the mayoralty
of the stern-visaged Steenwyck was a period of vigorous and systematic
administration in which the municipal government was coping continu-
ously and realistically with the needs of the community, and in which, by
implication at least, significant leadership was exercised by the mayor.[16]

As the mayoral year drew to a close Steenwyck apparently was not
available for another term (he died late in 1684, shortly after his retirement from office, and had perhaps been ill). In anticipation of the
governor's choice of his successor, the magistrates continued to exhibit
their interest in having the mayor, as well as the other magistrates, representative of the local will. The petitioners of November 9, 1683, had not
proposed the popular election of the mayor along with that of the aldermen, but they had requested that the governor and his council choose
the mayor from among the elected aldermen, thus ensuring a degree of
acceptability to the local electorate.

The magistrates acted only partly upon this principle in proposing a
successor to Steenwyck. They presented Dongan with a list of seven
nominees, only three of whom were among the elected magistrates. The
governor's choice nevertheless fell upon one of the three, Gabriel
Minvielle, a common councilman and a citizen long active in local affairs.
Though of French birth he had lived in Holland before migrating to
America. His wife was John Lawrence's daughter. In the ensuing year,
when the time came to appoint a new mayor, the magistrates reminded
the governor of his grant that the mayor would be appointed from among
the aldermen chosen by the freemen. To emphasize the point they ap-
pended the list of aldermen recently elected. However, Dongan chose
Nicholas Bayard, who was then completing a term as alderman, but who
was not among the recently elected group. Though Bayard was of Dutch
Huguenot background, he belonged to a faction of the local Dutch society
identified with a rising Anglo-Dutch elite. When the Dongan charter finally
was promulgated in 1686, it did not limit the governor's appointment of

the mayor except to make it subject to the advice of the governor's council.[17]

As far as the office of mayor was concerned, the Dongan charter of 1686 was significant chiefly for describing and confirming powers and practices which had existed in the office from its inception and which had been elaborated during Steenwyck's recent mayoralty. For example, it followed existing practice in specifying the "form and ceremony" to be followed in inducting the mayor and aldermen into office. The governor, "by and with the advice of his Council," was to appoint the mayor each year on the feast day of St. Michael the Archangel (September 29). The oath of office was to be administered on October 14, when the new administration would be installed. Whether this was as yet the ceremonious occasion it was to become before the end of the seventeenth century, the records do not reveal. But it already was the practice on the appointed day for the mayor, aldermen, and common councilmen to wait upon the governor and his council at the fort, where the new mayor was sworn in. The mayor, aldermen, and common councilmen then returned to the City Hall, where the new officers were called and sworn and the retiring officers dismissed.[18]

The charter also defined the powers of the city's chief executive—if this term is appropriate for an office that involved legislative and judicial, as well as administrative, duties. From the beginning, the mayor and aldermen had exercised both legislative and judicial functions, and as described in the Dongan charter the mayor's duties still were basically undifferentiated from those of the aldermen and common councilmen. The group as a whole sat together in common council to do most of the legislative and administrative work: to levy taxes, to authorize public improvements, and to enact orders for the public welfare—such as to decree practices "For the Due Observance of the Lords Day," limit the number of carters, set penalties for throwing garbage into the streets, require building permits so that "uniformity may be observed in the streets," establish market regulations, and provide for "hookes, ladders & Bucketts to be kept in Convenient Places, within this Citty for Avoyding the Perrill of fire." Periodically the mayor and aldermen decreed the assize and price of bread—in May 1684 this was set at "five Stivers Wampom Or One Penny halfe penny" for a thirteen-ounce loaf of white bread. At times the mayor and aldermen (but not the common councilmen) sat as a court. The charter empowered the mayor and recorder and three or more aldermen to hear cases of larceny, riots, routs, extortions, and the like, and to hold weekly a "Court of Common Pleas for all Actions of Debt Trespass . . . Ejectment and other Personal Actions."[19]

In all these activities the stated role of the mayor differed only slightly from that of the aldermen, although numerous special tasks might actually be assigned to him in implementing the orders of the municipal body. The presence of the mayor or his deputy was essential to a quorum in the legislative session, and either the mayor or the recorder (the city's legal adviser) was required to be present at sessions of the courts. In the areas of executive and administrative authority, the mayor shared many powers with the aldermen and councilmen, such as the administration of oaths and the admission of persons as freemen, a status prerequisite to the exercise of a trade or handicraft in the community. The one power that belonged exclusively to the mayor was that of granting licenses to tavern-keepers, victuallers, and retail liquor dealers. The mayor and the applicant were to agree on the sum, but the money was to go into the municipal coffers.[20]

On paper, then, it might appear that the office of mayor was not markedly more important than that of alderman or councilman. And this impression has been strengthened by the frequent turnover in the office in this early period. During the first generation of the office, there were thirteen different incumbents, twelve mayors, and one acting mayor. The term was annual, and few mayors held the office two years running, although several were reappointed at a later date. There is no evidence that the appointees sought the position; indeed in 1684 the magistrates decreed a fine of £20 to be levied on anyone who refused to act after he had been appointed.[21]

This implication of reluctance to serve can be interpreted as evidence that the mayoralty imposed considerable demands in time and effort. Neither this nor the characteristics of the men who held the office would suggest that New York City's first mayors were figureheads. Invariably they were merchant-leaders—often the most affluent—in the local society. All of them had had local administrative experience before assuming the mayoralty and all had been or ultimately were members of the governor's council.[22] That the governor recognized the mayoralty as important is apparent from the fact that he refused to relinquish his right of appointment to it and that he took pains to name as mayor men capable of exerting influence among the local citizens. The residents of the city were sufficiently aware of the power inherent in the office to press for methods of selection that would guarantee the mayor's acceptability to the community.

Despite the paucity of stated powers, the mayoralty was a position of consequence because of the leadership the incumbent exerted not only in serving the needs of the city and gaining advantage for it but also in winning community support for the provincial authority.

Thus in 1689, when the Leisler faction of the Dutch citizenry challenged the influence of the growing Anglo-Dutch elite in the city and colony—personified in Mayor Stephanus Van Cortlandt and ex-Mayor Nicholas Bayard—they, too, used the mayoralty to strengthen their precarious and transient hold on the city government. The Committee of Safety decreed the popular election of the mayor, and the voters chose for the office Dutch-born Peter Delanoy (New York's only elected mayor until 1834), who, since 1683, had had a continuous record of effective public service to the community—as assessor, treasurer, common councilman, and chamberlain, and who served as a member of Leisler's council.[23]

NOTES

1. For an earlier treatment of this theme, see Bayrd Still, "New York's Mayoralty: the Formative Years," *New-York Historical Society Quarterly*, 47 (July, 1963): 239-55. On the mayoralty in the seventeenth and eighteenth centuries, see Arthur E. Peterson, *New York as an Eighteenth Century Municipality prior to 1731* (New York, 1917) and George W. Edwards, *New York as an Eighteenth Century Municipality, 1731-1776* (New York, 1917). For the twentieth-century mayoralty, see Wallace S. Sayre and Herbert Kaufman, *Governing New York City* (New York, 1960), chap. 18.
2. E. B. O'Callaghan, ed., *Documentary History of the State of New York* (4 vols., Albany, 1849-51), 1: 602-4; William R. Shepherd, *The Story of New Amsterdam* (New York, 1926), pp. 181-94. New York was said to be "full fifteen hundred souls strong" at the time of the British conquest. By 1698, New York City and County numbered 4,937, according to an official census. Ira Rosenwaike, *Population History of New York City* (Syracuse, 1972), pp. 3, 7. Thomas J. Archdeacon, in *New York City, 1664-1710: Conquest and Change* (Ithaca, 1976), estimates that New York City was 80 percent Dutch in 1677 and still predominantly Dutch in 1703 (pp. 39, 45). For a survey of provincial politics in New York from 1664 to 1689, see Michael Kammen, *Colonial New York: A History* (New York, 1975), chaps. 4 and 5.
3. *Documentary History of New York*, 1: 600-2.
4. Ernest S. Griffith, *History of American City Government* (New York, 1938), pp. 226, 229; John R. Brodhead, *History of the State of New York* (2 vols., New York, 1871), 2:60, 76-77.
5. Elizur Y. Smith, "Captain Thomas Willett, First Mayor of New York," *New York History*, 21 (1940): 408-17; Brodhead, *History of the State of New York*, 2:28, 30, 45, 47, 76.
6. Willett served as mayor from June 12, 1665, through June 12, 1666. Delavall

is listed as mayor on June 13, 1666, through at least July 16, 1667. Presumably Willett resumed the post on July 23, 1667, retaining it at least through Aug. 4, 1668. Steenwyck is listed as mayor on Aug. 17, 1668. Berthold Fernow, ed., *The Records of New Amsterdam from 1653 to 1674* (7 vols., New York, 1897), 6: 15, 18, 85, 88, 141, 144. For Steenwyck, see *Dictionary of American Biography*, 17:559; D. T. Valentine, "Cornelis Steenwyck," *Manual of the Corporation of the City of New-York* (New York, 1864), pp. 648-64; John C. Webster, *Cornelis Steenwyck, Dutch Governor of Acadie*, a paper read at the annual meeting of the Canadian Historical Association, Ottawa, 1929 (privately printed, 1929), pp. 5-6. I am indebted to Dr. Jacob Judd for excerpts from "Exchequer, Queen's Remembrancer Port Books," now in the Public Record Office, London, which reveal Steenwyck's extensive trade through the port of Dover between 1677 and 1684.

7. Steenwyck served as mayor from August 14 (?), 1668 to Oct. 9, 1669, and by reappointment to Oct. 13, 1670. Thomas Delavall again became mayor on Oct. 13, 1670, and served until Oct. 13, 1671. Matthias Nicolls, the provincial secretary, served from Oct. 13, 1671, to Oct. 13 (?), 1672, and John Lawrence from Oct. 13 (?), 1672, to Aug. 17, 1673. For Nicolls, see *Dictionary of American Biography*, 13:514-15; Delancey Nicoll, *Matthias Nicolls, 1626-1687*, address delivered before the Colonial Dames of the State of New York, Jan. 21, 1915 (privately printed). Victor H. Paltsits, ed., *Minutes of the Executive Council of the Province of New York, Administration of Francis Lovelace, 1668-1673* (3 vols., Albany, 1910), 2:693; *Records of New Amsterdam*, 6:198-99, 201.

8. Shepherd, *Story of New Amsterdam*, pp. 198-208; Brodhead, *History of the State of New York*, 2:207-12, 222; *Documentary History of New York*, 1:609-10; Peterson, *New York prior to 1731*, p. 155; *Records of New Amsterdam*, 6:396-98; 7:113, 133-34; Webster, *Cornelis Steenwyck*, p. 5.

9. Jerome R. Reich, *Leisler's Rebellion: A Study of Democracy in New York, 1664-1720* (Chicago, 1953), pp. 20-31; Brodhead, *History of the State of New York*, 2:277, 289.

10. Matthias Nicolls served as mayor from Nov. 10, 1674, to Oct. 17, 1675; William Darvall, Dutch-born merchant and landowner, from Oct. 17, 1675, to Oct. 13 (?), 1676; Nicholas De Meyer, Dutch-born baker, miller, and merchant, from Oct. 13 (?), 1676, to Oct. 14, 1677; Stephanus Van Cortlandt, native-born merchant in the Holland and India trade, Oct. 14, 1677, to Oct. 14, 1678; Thomas Delavall from Oct. 14, 1678, to Nov. 21, 1679; Francis Rombouts, merchant of French Huguenot background, from Nov. 21, 1679, to Oct. 30, 1680; and William Dyer, English-born merchant and civil servant, long in the colonies, from Oct. 30, 1680, to Nov. 24, 1683. Before the close of his first term, Mayor Dyer, who was the collector of the customs, was sent to England to stand trial on treason charges brought against him because he had collected customs duties which had expired by limitation through Andros's failure to renew them. He cleared himself of the charges. During his prolonged absence, William Beekman served as deputy mayor, exercising the duties of office from Sep. 3, 1681, to Oct. (?), 1683. During this period the governor continued the incumbent officials in office; so Beekman's continuous tenure was longer than that of most mayors of the period. Steenwyck served from Nov. 24, 1683, to Oct. 14, 1684. He was succeeded by Gabriel Minvielle, Oct. 14, 1684, to Oct. 19 (?), 1685; Nicholas Bayard, who served two terms from at least Oct. 19, 1685, to Oct. 14, 1687, and Stephanus Van Cortlandt from Oct. 14, 1687, to Oct. 14, 1689. *Minutes of the Common Council of the City of New York, 1675-1776* (8 vols., New York, 1905), 8:145-46 (hereafter cited as *M.C.C.*).

11. Charles M. Andrews, *Colonial Self-Government, 1652-1689* (New York, 1904), p. 95; "Proceedings of the General Court of Assizes," *New-York*

Historical Society Collections (1912), pp. 14–16, 36; *Documents Relative to the Colonial History of the State of New-York* (15 vols., Albany, 1853–87), 3:334. Dongan arrived in New York on Aug. 25, 1683; and on Oct. 17 a representative assembly for the province of New York was convened, on Dongan's call. It drew up a charter of liberties and privileges, embodying the privileges for which the people had been agitating. James signed the charter on Oct. 14, 1684, but it never was delivered. After he became king, in 1685, he disavowed the charter and planned to incorporate the province of New York in the proposed Dominion of New England. When a new commission was sent to Dongan in 1686, no mention was made of a representation assembly, and all powers of legislation and taxation were vested in the governor and the council. The same fate did not befall the realization of representative government for New York City. Andrews, *Colonial Self-Government*, pp. 96–98.

12. *M.C.C.*, 1:104–5.
13. *Documents Relative to Colonial History of New-York*, 3:339; *M.C.C.*, 1:107. The incumbent aldermen were Johannes Van Brugh, James Graham, Samuel Wilson, Peter Jacob Marius, and John Lawrence. Dongan's appointees as aldermen (on Nov. 24, 1683), in addition to Bayard, included John Inians, William Pinhorne, Gulian Verplanck, John Robinson, and William Cox.
14. *M.C.C.*, 1:110–14.
15. Ibid., 1:115, 156–57. On Jan. 15, 1684, James Graham was appointed recorder, "to be Assistant to the Mayor and Aldermen in the Rule of Government of the said city and administration of justice in their Court of Record." Ibid., 1:117–18.
16. Ibid., 1:119–21, 123, 131, 141–42, 147, 149–50, 152–53.
17. Ibid., 1:157–59, 170–71.
18. Ibid., 1:159, 298–99, 182–83. As early as 1678, Governor Andros had referred to Oct. 14 as "the Usual tyme and Day of Elleccon." Ibid., 1:63–64. For later ceremony, see ibid., 1:385–86.
19. Ibid., 1:133–40, 150, 297, 304; Richard B. Morris, ed. *Select Cases of the Mayor's Court of New York City, 1674–1784* (Washington, D.C., 1935), p. 47; Peterson, *New York prior to 1731*, pp. 11, 24. Prior to the establishment of the Court of Quarter Sessions in 1683, the court had been constituted as the Court of Mayor and Aldermen or Sessions.
20. *M.C.C.*, 1:299, 301–2; Peterson, *New York prior to 1731*, pp. 16, 27.
21. Ibid., p. 35; *M.C.C.*, 1:157.
22. Cornelis Steenwyck, Nicholas De Meyer, Gabriel Minvielle, and John Lawrence were among the wealthiest men in the city, as was the father of Stephanus Van Cortlandt. Willett had been assistant governor of Plymouth Colony; Delavall had been receiver of shipping and alderman; Nicolls was secretary of the province in 1664 and was to be speaker of the first assembly in the province. Lawrence was appointed alderman in 1665, 1669, 1670, and 1671 before becoming mayor in 1672. Darvall and De Meyer were aldermen at various times. Van Cortlandt was schepen during the Dutch reconquest and later alderman. Rombouts served as schepen in 1674 and, both before and after, as alderman. Dyer was collector of the port; acting mayor Beekman had been schepen in New Orange; Minvielle was officer of a militia company and alderman; and Nicholas Bayard was provincial secretary under the Dutch reoccupation, as well as alderman, before his appointment as mayor. When Governor Dongan lacked a quorum in his council, he gave the oath to "Nicholas Bayard, the present Mayor, to serve . . . until his Ma'tys pleasure be known." *Documentary History of New York*, 1:189.
23. Delanoy, a merchant of Dutch Huguenot background, was a member of Leisler's Committee of Safety. He had been active in local government throughout the 1680s. The Committee of Safety authorized popular election

of the mayor as well as of other officers; the vote was announced on Oct. 7, 1689, and the selection was confirmed by Jacob Leisler on Oct. 14, the date on which the mayor traditionally was confirmed by the governor's appointment. *M.C.C.*, 1:206-7. In referring to the election of "Peter De Lanoy Mayor" and others by "majority of voices" of "all the *Protestant* freeholders of this County," the critics of Leisler asserted that they did not object "so much" to the persons as to the "method of their being chosen; neither shall we be offended if it shall please his Majesty to add unto our former priviledges this likewise." "A Modest and Impartial Narrative of several Grievances . . . that the Peaceable and Most Considerable Inhabitants of . . . New York Lye under, By the . . . Arbitrary Proceedings of Jacob Leysler and his Accomplices," *Documents Relative to Colonial History of New York*, 3:675. The ethnic implications of New York City politics in connection with the Leisler movement are well developed by Thomas J. Archdeacon in his *New York City, 1664-1710: Conquest and Change*, and in his doctoral dissertation, "The Age of Leisler: New York City, 1689-1710," Columbia University, 1971. See also Kammen, *Colonial New York*, pp. 118-27.

EDWARD PESSEN

2

POLITICAL DEMOCRACY AND THE
DISTRIBUTION OF POWER
IN ANTEBELLUM NEW YORK CITY

Political democracy or something closely akin to it was substantially achieved in New York City during the second quarter of the nineteenth century. The democratization of local government had taken a great stride forward as early as 1804, when the state legislature had removed the freehold suffrage requirement and again in 1822 when "five dollar taxpayers" were made eligible for councilmanic elections. Another reform in that year transferred the selection of the mayor from the governor and the state senators, who composed the State Council of Appointments, to the popularly elected city council. In 1834 the people were finally given the power to choose the mayor in annual elections, in accord with the provisions of the charter reform of 1830. The democratic spirit of that reform was indicated too by the severe limits it placed on the city's chief executive in his dealings with the local legislature. An act of 1842 not only reduced the residency requirement for the city's voters but essentially did away with all property requirements. And the charter reform of 1849 provided that the nine heads of the city's executive departments were henceforth to be elected by the people rather than appointed by the common council. These charter reforms were themselves initiated by popularly elected delegates to charter conventions and had subsequently been put to popular referendums for approval.[1]

The right of almost all citizens not only to vote but to hold the highest municipal offices in New York, as in other cities, perhaps more than any other development accounts for the long-standing reputation of the period as the "era of the common man." It was widely believed both by contemporaries and by later scholars that the political rights won by commoners during the era gave them the lion's share of influence and power in their communities. A tyranny of the majority allegedly prevailed in Jacksonian America.

The purpose of this paper is to try to determine whether or not ordinary people truly dominated antebellum New York City and, if they did not, to discover which group or groups did in fact do so. This essay makes no claim to offering definitive conclusions about a question of such magnitude and complexity. Its author's more modest hope is that his observations may offer useful suggestions as to the directions future research and discussion might take.

New York City was of course in many respects an atypical urban community. Yet there is no reason to dismiss out of hand the distribution of power in the great metropolis as though it had no bearing on the situation in smaller towns and cities. We have recently discovered that there was an amazing degree of similarity in the social patterns and political systems of the nation's cities, whatever their sizes, populations, and geographical area.[2] If antebellum New York City was not the nation, the very fact that it was a city appears to have meant that its social and political developments would not be totally unlike those in other urban milieus. Scholars who would ascertain the sources of influence and power elsewhere must of course gather information on communities other than New York City. Such scholars would be well advised however to ponder the evidence concerning the nation's largest and wealthiest city.

Although historians and social scientists have often treated power as though it is manifested primarily, if not exclusively, in political institutions and political behavior, power can be revealed too in actions having nothing directly to do with politics. In view of the complexity of the phenomenon, not to mention the subjectivity of all scholarly attempts to define it, there is much to be said for Robert A. Dahl's suggestion that power is "a concept that seems highly useful as long as one does not demand that it be defined." In the same vein, the political scientist Raymond E. Wolfinger reports that "much useful research relevant to one aspect or another of power does not even use the term . . . and little seems to be lost by the omission."[3] Guided by these sensible observations, the discussion that follows will not essay yet another definition of the elusive concept but rather follow popular usage. Power, as we all know, involves the capacity in those who possess it to have their own way and/or to compel others either to do their bidding or to acquiesce in it. Further, power is internally differentiated; that is, there is power and power. Some forms are of great social importance, as when they touch on the vital affairs of large numbers of people, others are relatively insignificant, concerning only a few individuals in an essentially trivial respect (as would be the case, say, in a housewife's "power" over her family's menu).

In this essay power will be made operational by locating it in influential social and economic as well as political institutions of the antebellum city. If the search for power in its political manifestation will be dealt with swiftly, it is because that investigation has recently been publicly discussed, albeit in an admittedly less than exhaustive treatise.[4] In order to place the great city's distribution of social and economic power in clearer perspective, it does appear useful to draw attention to some of the more salient characteristics of its political life in the antebellum decades, in part on the basis of fresh evidence.[5]

For all their right to occupy as well as vote for local office, ordinary men were conspicuous in antebellum city government in their absence from it. Place was won not by the laborers, artisans, and clerks, the men of little property who predominated numerically in the city, but by men of the high prestige occupations who were in the top percentiles of wealth holding. From Philip Hone in 1826 to Caleb S. Woodhull in 1850 the mayor's office was occupied by an unbroken succession of eminent and wealthy merchants and attorneys, with the exception of James Harper, who was mayor in 1844, a highly successful publisher. The transfer of the selection from the city council to the people was accompanied by no shift in the socioeconomic status of New York City's mayors. It remained an exalted one.

The council, consisting of an alderman and assistant alderman from each of the city's changing number of wards,[6] was also composed disproportionately of businessmen, professionals, and great wealth holders. In contrast to the mayors, whose social backgrounds remained intact throughout the era, the social profile of councilmen did undergo a modest but significant change. For the first half of the quarter century, 1825 to 1837/8, merchants and other businessmen constituted about 50 percent of the total, attorneys and professionals 25 percent, grocers and other probable retailers about 15 percent, and artisans—some of whom were actually entrepreneurs—about 10 percent. No laborers were to be found in the council, nor were they present during the second half of the period.

In the later years the business contingent was if anything slightly enlarged, but the percentage of professionals declined to 15, while that of artisans and artisan entrepreneurs rose to 16 or 17 percent. A more dramatic decline after 1838 took place in the number of very wealthy and very eminent men of Old Family in the council.

The rich,[7] who made up about two-thirds of the body in 1826, dropped to one-half in 1831, to about two-fifths in 1840, and to one-quarter by mid-century. Since we are here considering the wealthiest 1 or 2 percent of adults in the community, the last faction is substantial enough, indicating that money continued to be heavily overrepresented in local government. As for the city's most ancient or respected elite families, they were at no time heavily represented. A sprinkling of Motts, Schieffelins, Nevinses, and Roosevelts of the 1820s and early 1830s was matched by Bensons, Van Schaicks, Ingrahams, and Ogdens in the 1840s.

If poor men were totally missing from the halls of local government throughout the period 1825–50, rich men sat in diminishing numbers, while the crême de la crême offered handfuls of token representatives. The swells evidently felt they had better uses for their time.[8]

It seems clear that the declining representation of the rich and the eminent in the local legislature was a matter of their own choice, in refusing to offer themselves as candidates in the same numbers, rather than a voter rebellion against them. This would explain why in 1828, when perhaps one-half the council were rich men, only about a half dozen belonged to the set that Miss Lydia Kane called the "true elite." And yet, when it was decided that a charter revision should be presented in 1830 for the first time in almost a century, members of the best families bestirred themselves: here was an issue befitting personages of their rank. Despite the fact that seventy convention delegates were to be elected in separate ward elections, five from each ward, and that the preponderance of inhabitants of almost all the wards were poor men, the rich and the eminent won 80 percent of the convention seats. Delegates included Peter Augustus Jay, Robert Bogardus, John Hone, Lambert Suydam, Evert Bancker, Effingham Schieffelin, Cornelius Schuyler, and others of similarly great wealth and renown.[9]

Age of democracy or no, ordinary men neither ran for nor won local office. It used to be thought that an important explanation of their non-involvement was the fact that poor or modestly situated men could not spare the time for political work that was without pay. If this were in fact the reason, it would only indicate the political impotence of the "lower orders" in acquiescing to a system that denied them participation in governing. Since, however, in New York as in other cities, the councils often met no more than once or twice a month and then at night, it seems clear that it was reasons other than their alleged inability to attend sessions that account for the near exclusion of working people and members of the lower middle classes from city government. As an office that paid the then princely sum of between $2,000 and $3,000 per annum, in addition to providing valuable perquisites, the mayoralty must have seemed extremely attractive to ordinary men of little wealth. And yet, at no point in the "era of the common man" was the post ever filled by a commoner. Whether due to the continued deference they showed their social superiors, their certainty of defeat, or other reasons, ordinary men rarely held or offered themselves for local office during the period traditionally named in their honor.

This essay is concerned exclusively with power on the local level. It is nevertheless a matter of interest that at a time, in the 1840s, when the representation of rich men in the city legislature had shrunk to its lowest point, they constituted about one-half the city's congressional delegation. In attempting to explain the "pervasive" political power of the city's wealthy merchants in Congress, a modern student attributes it in part to the fact that "they held many of the legislative seats, but also [to] their allegiance with other interest groups with whom they shared similar viewpoints, thereby assuring absolute political control."[10]

Political power is reflected more clearly perhaps in the actions of government than in the socioeconomic characteristics of the men who occupy it. For it is conceivable that the wealthy men who hold office might legislate in the interests of the mass of have-nots, in part out of fear that their failure to do so would get them turned out of office. According to the traditional interpretation, in which supposedly the masses ruled in Tocquevillean America as does the deity over the universe, politics here followed precisely such a pattern. Their own absence from the halls of government was thus not a sign of the political powerlessness of the masses. The question then concerns the character of New York City's political enactments during the period: did they serve, were they designed to serve the interests of the common man?[11]

Thousands of ordinances were passed by the city council during the era. Perhaps because they were concerned primarily with such undramatic themes as garbage disposal, water supply, police and fire protection, street cleaning and maintenance, lighting, and regulation of markets, these measures have been largely ignored by some urban historians. The "new urban history" that is all the vogue is preoccupied with sociological themes.[12] An important task of historians of nineteenth-century New York City is to examine far more closely than heretofore the legislative behavior of the city council, in order to determine the political and social philosophies underlying its enactments, as well as the interests that were best served by these bills. From the substantial evidence that has to date been unearthed, it does seem that the city was governed largely for, as well as by, its large propertied interests.

Tax rates were low because wealthy taxpayers insisted that they be. Budgets were therefore minuscule, pitifully inadequate to cope with the onrushing problems faced by the city in an age of unprecedented over-crowding, ethnic and racial tensions, and pervasive inequality. For that matter, the city's tax assessors looked the other way at flagrant under-assessments perpetrated above all by the great wealth holders. Whether they had to do with a fresh water supply, innovations in sewage disposal, or the introduction of a professional "London-style" police force, improvements of every sort were made available first to residents of the more exclusive residential districts and neighborhoods. Some of the city's most valuable real estate in the form of wharves and "water grants" was leased by the city council on easy terms or sold cheaply to members of the Astor, Bowne, Colden, Goelet, Havemeyer, Lexon, Lorillard, Roosevelt, and Schermerhorn families. Lucrative privileges were regularly solicited by—and granted to—wealthy owners and lessees from these and similarly wealthy and prestigious families.[13]

Observing these and other instances of the conservative social bias underlying the policies first of the Common Council, then of the Board of Aldermen, a contemporary New Yorker attributed them to the fact that "nearly every alderman has in some degree owed his success to the personal efforts and influence of 'backers,' who must be recompensed for their services. This recompense sometimes consists in a return of political assistance."[14] Evidence is lacking to confirm the charge that New York City's legislators engaged in a "payoff" by enacting laws sought by their wealthy supporters. Such evidence is not necessary, however, to sustain a more significant generalization: whatever their motives, the city's officials showed far greater sensitivity to the interests of the great property owners than to the interests of any other socioeconomic group. It does not seem unreasonable to conclude that deference by government to a particular social group bespeaks the great power of that group.

Political power is also manifested negatively in what government fails to do.[15] The reluctance of the city government to confront the plethora of problems pressing in on its poorer residents, the niggardly expenditures assumed for social welfare purposes, for example, point to the relative powerlessness of the ordinary citizens who stood to benefit from such policies.[16] Of course laissez-faire on the level of municipal government appears to have been an article of faith of the antebellum period. It can well be asked, however, why the principle was so selectively applied, for certainly it did not inhibit governmental intervention on behalf of the most prosperous citizens. Both the action and the inaction of antebellum New York City government testified to the inordinate power enjoyed by the small number of the city's rich, on the one hand, and to the lack of power possessed by the mass of residents, on the other.

If the preceding discussion has paid no attention to the party preferences that divided New Yorkers, it is primarily because major party labels, whether Democratic, National Republican, or Whig, seemed to have slight significance on the level of municipal politics. Certainly voters became terribly exercised, in some cases cracking heads and resorting to other forms of violence at the polls, in deciding which party would carry the day. Party propaganda, particularly when publicized by the Jacksonians, stressed the dedication of candidates and officeholders to the great mass of voters. Party performance invariably failed to live up to party pronouncements. Similarly conservative policies were followed by the Democrats and Tammany as by their major party opponents, in part, no doubt, because the wealth and standing of such Tammany leaders as Gideon Lee, George Templeton Strong, Preserved Fish, Walter Bowne, Stephen Allen, John Treat Irving, and Jonathan Coddington, were similar to the wealth and standing of elitist Whig leaders in the city.[17]

It had been not long ago asserted that the allegedly overwhelming preference of the city's richest men for the Whig party in the aftermath of the Bank War of the 1830s testified to the fears the Democracy inspired in the city's "men of quality."[18] It is of course conceivable that wealthy New Yorkers might have preferred the Whigs to the Democrats by a very great margin but on the basis of very slight differences that they discerned between the parties. The point appears to have been made moot by recent disclosures which demonstrate that in fact there was "an almost even division" in the major party preferences of the city's wealthiest merchants before, during, and after the Bank War.[19] Extant evidence suggests that if the major parties appealed to ordinary citizens for their mass voting support, they relied on the atypically wealthy for their leadership.

Several minor parties that flourished briefly in New York City during the Jackson years had reputations for social radicalism. In the case of the Locofocos—actually dissident Democrats who broke with Tammany for a short period between 1835 and 1837—the reputation was undeserved, nourished and kept alive by Whigs who were eager to identify the Locofocos with the orthodox Jacksonians and to censure the alleged radicalism of both.[20] To judge from its platform, the other group, the Working Men's party of the late 1820s and early 1830s, was indeed radical.[21] The trouble with these factions was that they never came close to winning a citywide election or taking over City Hall. While the Working Men were supported at the polls by few workers, many of the party's positions were clearly in the interests of both laborers and skilled artisans. The failure of such a program to achieve success in antebellum New York City points to the relative powerlessness of those whom it was designed to serve.

To achieve a deeper grasp of political power in the city it would be invaluable to have more information on the operations of the city's judicial system. One wishes to know to what extent the flagrant bias demonstrated by Judge Edwards against the journeymen tailors in the famous conspiracy trial of 1836 was typical of judicial behavior during the period. A fruitful line of future enquiry would examine carefully the procedures for selecting judges, their social backgrounds and philosophies, and above all the tenor of their findings, with the end in view of interpreting the results of such research in terms of the questions posed by this essay. When we have such knowledge, in addition to detailed new evidence on the public behavior and the private thinking of mayors, aldermen, and other officials, we shall be in a position to speak with greater assurance about the distribution of political power in antebellum New York City.

Power was not confined to, let alone monopolized by, City Hall. One of the recurrent themes of recent urban historiography is that New York and other cities dealt most hesitantly and ineptly with the host of problems thrown up by industrialization and immigration. Whatever the theoretical powers city government may have had available to it, mayors and councils in fact opted for timidity if not evasion in coping with the complex issues of the time.[22] In so doing, the political powers-that-were showed their lack of interest in the needs of the mass of persons who would have benefited from positive governmental action. For whatever reasons, responsibility for such vital matters as education for the children of the less than wealthy, poverty, social welfare broadly construed, artistic and intellectual culture for the masses, and a wide range of benevolent enterprises was assumed not by government, primarily, but by voluntary associations composed of private citizens.

Much work has been done by scholars on the leaderships and the activities of these organizations.[23] In his marvelous paean to the American "rage to associate," Alexis de Tocqueville had interpreted the era's voluntary associations as popular bodies through which American commoners achieved a strength in numbers that they lacked as individuals.[24] As was often the case, Tocqueville's conclusions owed more to logical inference than to factual evidence. The data unearthed by modern research do not sustain Tocqueville's surmises. True, ordinary men of little wealth and standing did join together in local self-help and fraternal societies, not to mention trades unions of the period. The associations concerned with broad public purposes, however, were not for them. Almost without exception New York City's most significant and influential voluntary associations were dominated by the city's upper crust of wealth and status.

The Humane Society of New York City, established originally to relieve the plight of imprisoned debtors, had by the Jacksonian era taken on additional tasks concerned with ameliorating the lot of prisoners and of the poor in general. Its managers were overwhelmingly businessmen and professionals, most of whose names appear on a list of the city's wealthiest men. The New York Association for Improving the Condition of the Poor was formed in 1843 "for the purpose of controlling the evils growing out of almsgiving, which encouraged idleness and led to crime." It sought to accomplish this purpose by discouraging begging and by inculcating habits of "frugality, temperance, industry, and self-dependence" in the "deserving poor." It disseminated material succor—never money—and moral advice to the needy, teaching them that the poor were the authors of their own misery. All of this association's chief officers and half of its elected board of managers belonged to the city's elite of wealth. As for the New York Society for the Prevention of Pauperism, which attributed poverty not to social conditions or institutions but to the ignorance, idleness, and intemperance of the poor, its chief officers were of the eminent Clarkson, Livingston, Murray, and Fish families, and most of its managers belonged to the city's richest wealth holders. Its successor, the New York Society for the Reformation of Juvenile Delinquents, supervised the House of Refuge, which taught youthful offenders that learning "habits of industry" was the path to future success. The historian of this association finds that its wealthy directors were a "self-perpetuating group" who "chose their replacements from others of like backgrounds."[25] I have discovered that during the second quarter of the nineteenth century two-thirds of the society's managers belonged to the city's wealthiest five hundred.

It is not simply that most managers, directors, or officers of these social welfare bodies were wealthy and socially eminent. The fact is that at any time in the antebellum decades most of that larger body I have called the rich—persons who were among the city's top five or ten hundred wealth holders—made it their business to participate actively in such associations. Their motives, as impossible to know with certainty as are those of other men, seem to have been varied. Some historians stress "social control," narrowly construed as the chief incentive for their activism. My own belief is that their feelings were more complex, with noblesse oblige, civic pride, Christian morality, among others, intermingling with other and more realistic objectives. The important question, however, concerns not their motives but the pattern of their public behavior. It is hardly a strained reading of the evidence to conclude that the city's socioeconomic elite used their leadership of influential voluntary associations to promote their own interests.

Surely it was in their interest to show the needy that somebody, particularly their social betters, cared, as it was in their interest too, to prevent the bottom from falling out altogether, inevitably exacerbating social tensions in the community. It is conceivable that as the have-nots were fed, clothed, and sheltered their minds might have been nourished by the social message congenial to Thomas Skidmore, Frances Wright, and other of the city's radicals, which stressed society's culpability for the existence of poverty.[26] That the poor were rather indoctrinated with variations on the Malthusian theme that social misery was due to individual, never to institutional, failings, perhaps better than anything else reflected the power of the elitists, who, in controlling the city's welfare institutions, also controlled their propaganda. Both by their deeds and their pronouncements the city's voluntary associations revealed their determination to maintain the amazingly inequitable status quo of the time.[27] Whatever power these organizations possessed—and it was great if ultimately impossible to measure—was a power held and used by the rich and socially prestigious men who managed and directed them.

Rivaling if not surpassing in importance the voluntary associations that served the needy and destitute were those concerned with the mind of the larger community. Such an organization was the Free School Society, which after 1825 became the Public School Society. Under the one name or the other the body controlled public education in New York City during the first half of the nineteenth century. Noting that most of the society's trustees throughout the period were merchants, financiers, and manufacturers, with all of the rest lawyers or doctors, the modern historian of the agency concludes that it "attracted the services of many wealthy men." In fact, spot checks for the years 1828 and 1841 disclose that between 60 and 65 percent of more than a hundred trustees belonged to the city's wealthiest families.

The repository for most of the era for state funds for the city's schools, the society controlled a system that ultimately included seventy-four schools which provided free schooling for children "of all classes." The society's formal objectives, as stated in many reports it published, provide a useful clue to the social beliefs of its managers. The great value of education was "to prepare for usefulness a large portion of the population who might otherwise grow up in idleness, remain a burden on the community, and become victims of every species of vice and profligacy incident to extensive and populous cities." It hoped that schools under its influence would foster "feelings of independence, which [were] highly important to cultivate, and be promoted among [the] poor and laboring classes."[28] In an age when Horace Mann never ceased reminding New England manufacturers that public schools would make working class children more industrious and productive or when the wealthy Samuel Breck could advise his fellow Philadelphians that children of the poorer classes—once educated—could rise to the very pinnacle of society,[29] the doctrine propagated by the School Society was evidently popular not in New York City alone. That these ideas were in a sense fashionable elsewhere detracts not at all from their significance for the great metropolis. Public education was controlled there by members of the city's socioeconomic upper crust, who used their great power among other ways by fostering a social ideology conducive to strengthening the social order under which they thrived.

Education was not confined to the public schools. Such organizations of the period as the Athenaeum, which sponsored public lectures, as did the Stuyvesant Institute, various private libraries, and the Clinton Hall Association, which concentrated on promoting the "moral and intellectual improvement of the merchants' clerks," also played an important part in the intellectual life of the city. About 75 percent of the leaders of these organizations were members of the city's wealthiest and most eminent families. The elite leadership of these and the city's artistic and cultural associations comported themselves as they did in their other activities, always with an eye toward inducing the beneficiaries of their largesse to look kindly on society's present arrangements, to regard failure as the wages of sin, and to believe that personal betterment would result only from hard work and acceptance of appropriate social values—that is, the values propagated by the elite.

Minds were molded by many sources during the era. It would be useful to conduct a research into the backgrounds as well as the social philosophies of the city's newspaper publishers and editors in order to determine the extent to which the wealth and conservatism of such men as Moses Yale Beach, James Gordon Bennett, James Watson Webb, Charles King, Mordecai Noah, and the Tappan brothers were typical of the profession in the antebellum era.[30] A close but admittedly impressionistic look at editorial pages indicates that the city's journals regularly disseminated comforting and conservative social pronouncements to their readerships, assuring them that in this blessed country even the "humble mechanic" had access to "all the facilities in business and every means of gaining independence which are extended only to rich monopolists in England." George Henry Evans in the *Working Man's Advocate,* the journal of the Working Men's party, and *The Man,* the organ of the city's unions, editorialized very differently, but one has good reason to suspect that Evans's radicalism was atypical of antebellum New York City journalism. From what we know at present, it would be altogether unsurprising if by far the greater number and the most widely read of the city's journals were published by uncommonly wealthy men who sold conservative ideology in addition to (largely mercantile) news, partisan (major) party politics, and advertising space.

Another matter deserves mention, although for obvious reasons it too will be only glanced at in this paper. Religious institutions commanded a great if unmeasurable power over the minds and actions of the city's residents. The question is not so much whether ministers and priests were wealthy men, for all the interest in Jay Dolan's recent disclosures that the city's Irish Catholic priests, for example, had unusually high incomes and perquisites which enabled many of them "to live luxuriously."[31] Religious man above all others lives not by bread alone. The important questions concern the character of the churches' social teachings and the extent to which these teachings were influenced by or bespeak the power of those elements in the community they best served. It is instructive that the religious movement that perhaps reached the widest audience and touched them more deeply than did any other, Charles G. Finney's evangelicalism, was enthusiastically supported by the rich and eminent. In his own memoirs Finney observed that his appeal took "effect very generally among the influential classes." New York City's wealthy merchants not only themselves attended the special morning services Finney set aside for them, but they also gave their clerks time off to attend Finney's meetings.[32] Finney's chief financial support came from some of the city's most successful merchants, men like Anson G. Phelps, William E. Dodge, Arthur and Lewis Tappan. Such men were themselves religious zealots but the fact that, as one historian of Finney's movement has noted, it did not "threaten the economic underpinnings of society," helps explain the enthusiasm some nonzealots among the privileged orders felt for the new revivalism.

Wealthy Christians who had little sympathy for the "second Awakening" cast their lot with a religious enterprise, the social values of which were at least as conservative as those of Finney's movement. This was the "benevolent empire," the series of interdenominational mission, tract, Bible, and Sunday school societies that lay Protestants created during the era to spread the faith and deepen its hold on the minds and hearts of Americans. Clifford Griffin, the leading historian of this movement, has shown its profoundly conservative social biases. If it stressed the doctrine of the "contented poor," it did so primarily because its leaders "believed that they [themselves] would suffer if men playing lesser roles . . . did not respect their economic and social obligations."[33] Wherever these organizations were established they were led by men of prestigious occupation. New York City can accurately be described as the center of the movement. Roughly half the New Yorkers who sat as managers of the American Bible Society were of the city's richest families, as were more than two-thirds of the life members of the New York Bible Society, a branch of national organization. Similarly wealthy were most of the leaders of the American Tract Society and the American Board of Commissioners for Foreign Missions, both based in the city.

Philip Hone's manuscript diary, that goldmine of detailed information on every aspect of the social lives of the interurban elite, reveals that the lay leaders of the Episcopal church and Trinity Church in New York City were at the pinnacle of its economy and society. It would be interesting to look closely at the city's other denominations and churches in order to gather information on the character and backgrounds of their lay leadership.[34] Clearly much work remains to be done on this elusive subject before we can speak with any assurance about it. Yet from the not insignificant evidence accumulated to date, it appears that religion, like other of New York City's most influential institutions, was to an extraordinary extent dominated by wealthy and prestigious men. The power embodied in and wielded by churches, vestries, and lay benevolent organizations is power of a most complex sort, difficult if not impossible to disentangle, beyond the reach of the most refined quantitative methodology.[35] To sort out first the role of money and prestige in so spiritual an enterprise and then the influence of religion on the feelings and the behavior of laities is an intellectual challenge of the first order. It is nevertheless a task well worth undertaking, for in performing it sensibly we can gain far deeper insight than we presently have into how a massive if unmeasurable form of power was allocated.

Marxism regards "economic power" as the ultimate power, control over which enables those who possess it to exercise control over all other aspects of community life. One of the problems with this famous theory is its treatment of what is only an assumption as though it were a demonstrated fact—oftentimes a most sensible assumption, true, but an assumption nevertheless, particularly when it is offered to explain power in communities that have not yet been studied empirically. The approach used here is a different one. Assuming no necessary or invariable connection between economic and other forms of power, this section will simply ask: who or what groups controlled or dominated antebellum New York City's wealth, its credit, its economy in general? One need not be a Marxist to understand that power over economic institutions is a great power indeed.

Wealth, as I have shown elsewhere, was most inequitably distributed in nineteenth-century New York City, with the maldistribution becoming more skewed with the passage of time.[36] Modern estimates focus on the distribution of income, since data on wealth are not available from the official records. In the antebellum period it was different. The city's tax assessors were given the task of estimating the value of the personal property owned by every one of the city's residents, as well as the value of the real property they owned within the city. Unfortunately, New York's officials, unlike Boston's, did not publish lists of property owners and their estimated worth. Fortunately, it was possible first to create such lists, by recording every single notation made by the assessors in their notebooks as they went from house to house and lot to lot, and then to work out who owned every penny's worth of the city's property and how much and what proportion of the total they owned.[37] Lists of taxpayers created for 1828 and 1845 made it possible to discern changing trends in the distribution of the city's wealth.

The figures are of course marred by the notorious underassessments of wealth that were accepted by city officials. The fact that the prime beneficiaries of the underassessments were the greatest wealth holders suggests that the degree of inequality was actually greater or worse than the records indicate. The disclosed maldistribution is glaring enough.

In 1828 the wealthiest 1 percent of the city's adults owned about 40 percent of the city's wealth, while the next richest 3 percent of wealth holders held an additional 20 percent. By 1845 the richest 1 percent owned about half the wealth, with the richest 4 percent worth more than 80 percent of the total. The laborers, artisans, clerks, and petty shopkeepers who composed the mass of the city's population owned a minuscule proportion of its wealth. The mere figures do not suggest nearly so forcefully as does impressionistic or qualitative evidence the essential accuracy of Philip Hone's grim observation that New York City at midcentury had "arrived at the state of society to be found in the large cities of Europe," in which "the two extremes of costly luxury in living, expensive establishments and improvident waste are presented in daily and hourly contrast with squalid misery and hopeless destitution."[38]

That it is a truism detracts from neither the force nor the significance of the fact that money or wealth determines the quality and the costliness of the life one leads. Transmuting this cliché into the language of this paper, the "power" individuals have to live attractive or depressing material lives depends entirely on the wealth they own or have access to. In view of the importance to people as to whether they live at one level or another, what kind of space, housing, furniture, health facilities, clothing, food, leisure, are available to them and their families, it does not seem unreasonable or exaggerated to conclude that the power possession of money conferred over these goods was in a sense the power of powers. In New York City as elsewhere a tiny fragment of the population monopolized the power to live the good life. I have in an earlier publication spelled out in some detail the opulence of the lives led by the city's wealthiest families.[39] Ordinary people lived quite differently. The labor press of the era emphasized the abysmal housing and general living conditions of working people. A number of more comfortably situated observers agreed with the grim verdict of the labor radicals. In Horace Greeley's "deliberate estimate, the result of much enquiry," the two-thirds of the city's population who worked with their hands for a living commanded only a "pittance," with "each person [barely] subsisting thereon."[40] David Hosack, the great society doctor, and the humanitarian John H. Griscom both spoke of the absence of light, air, space, and sanitary facilities in the appalling housing conditions suffered by workers.[41] Class affected, in addition, the kind of schooling New Yorkers received, the theatres—if any—that they attended, their medical treatment and their relative immunity to cholera and other diseases, even the very smells permeating their neighborhoods, since (as John Duffy has shown) sewage improvements were introduced last, long after the period under discussion, in stench-ridden working-class areas where they were most needed.[42]

During the era poorer citizens were regularly regaled with assurances that either they or their children had ample opportunity—or "power"—to move up the economic scale. In fact very few made the leap from rags to riches.[43] It is likely that greater numbers made significant if less dramatic moves upward, from poverty to modest competencies. Evidence on the latter trend, however, is lacking. The amazing extent to which the rich of early in the century held on to or enhanced their fortunes through all vicissitudes, particularly great financial panics, points to the great power of inheritance laws, abetted by the exclusive social world inhabited by the rich and eminent, to perpetuate both the wealth of the leading families and the vastness of the gulf separating them from all others.[44]

In view of the inordinate proportion of the city's wealth that was commanded by a small number of families, it is hardly surprising to find that the city's banks, its insurance and marine insurance companies, its various corporations and business enterprises, were monopolized by these same families. It is conceivable that rich New Yorkers could have been assessed for personal wealth or estate, most of which had resulted from economic involvements outside the city, with the city's financial institutions owned by a great number of small investors. That was not the case, however. The very wealthiest New Yorkers, men such as John Jacob and William Astor, John G. Coster, Isaac Lawrence, George and Peter Lorillard, Nathaniel Prime, Nicholas W. and Peter G. Stuyvesant, James Lenox, William Rhinelander, Stephen Whitney, and Peter Goelet, were precisely the men who held offices and sat on the boards of directors of its great financial and commercial institutions.[45] The power of these organizations was great indeed.

Banking officials controlled the credit that was indispensable to the

growth of a youthful capitalistic economy, through their discount committees in effect determining who or what individuals got how much and at
what rates.[46] Moses Y. Beach, whose dubious contemporary lists of the
city's "wealthy men" were based on his actual ignorance both of the men
and their business affairs, concluded that the rich had little interest in
finance, since contemporary city directories rarely described them as
bankers. The occupational designations in the directories were misleading.[47] Actually, most of the city's wealthiest men were engaged in
finance, among their manifold business activities, and like John Jacob
Astor and Isaac Bronson in New York, Nathan Trotter in Philadelphia,
and the Brown Brothers in Baltimore, understood just how marvelously
lucrative such investments could be. Control over the lifeblood of business
enterprise gave to those who enjoyed it great power as well as profit.

If one is going to belabor the (economic) obvious, he should either do
so exhaustively, quantitatively, leaving nothing to the imagination, tracing
out comprehensively who owned how much of what, detailing how and
to what extent such ownership gave those who enjoyed it influence and
control over others, once and for all setting forth all the necessary data, or
he should do so, as I intend to in this context, glancingly and suggestively.
Perhaps because of their very obviousness, the essentials appear to have gone
largely unremarked by scholars. The rich and the great merchants were to
a great extent overlapping if not identical groups in New York City. In
addition to monopolizing wealth and credit, they controlled the city's
commerce. These were the "merchant capitalists" who during the era
took control of the small shop manufacturing process that enrolled most
of the city's skilled and semi-skilled artisans, whether masters or journeymen. As owners of most of the city's lots and real estate, they owned the
land on which people lived, in effect determining the price of both working people's housing and their labor. Trades unions of mechanics must of
course be entered into the equation of economic power. For all the great
number of crafts that organized and the strikes they waged, the brief life
span of the New York City labor movement before mid-century—from
1833 to 1837—and the ephemerality of its wage and hours gains suggest
that its power was slight.[48]

It would be useful to have a fuller picture than we now have of who or
which group of New Yorkers controlled the various facets and forms of
economic power. Present evidence, however, is far from insubstantial. It
indicates that power over the most important branches of the city's
economy had been engrossed by a small number of extraordinarily
wealthy men and families.

The insufficiency and the qualitative inadequacies of the evidence accumulated to date require scholars to do a great deal of additional research before we can presume to offer final answers to the question posed at the outset of this essay. And yet our present evidence, if not definitive, is substantial and compelling. It indicates that the achievement of political democracy (at least for white males) did not mean that ordinary people of modest property assumed power over their communities. Certainly they did not do so in antebellum New York City. And as was noted earlier, in view of the remarkable similarity in the social patterns of antebellum cities, whatever their size and location, there is reason to suspect that the maldistribution of power in New York may not have been unique.

During the period that we used to call the "era of the common man," political and other forms of power appear to have been distributed as unequally as was wealth. Power of every sort seemed to fall into the hands not of the mass of commoners but rather of a small number of uncommonly rich and eminent men. While these men and their families moved in a social world inhabited almost exclusively by their own sort, evidence is lacking that they were a tight clique who sought only to promote the interests and power of their own class or that they even thought of themselves as constituting a homogeneous class. The "state" in New York City was not quite the "executive committee of the ruling class," nor did the rich and eminent appear to regard themselves as a bourgeoisie of similar interests. Brian Danforth has shown the extent to which differing economic activities and interests also divided the city's great merchants politically.[49] That the Marxist theory of the state, literally defined, is not demonstrated by the evidence for New York City, however, does not mean that the Tocquevillean thesis that commoners dominated and had power over antebellum America is sustained.

A modern urban historian concludes, on the basis of impressionistic political and social evidence, that the New York City socioeconomic elite "considered the whole city subject to its general supervision."[50] The argument of this paper is that while evidence on the beliefs of this elite is inconclusive, impressive if incomplete evidence indicates that they exercised not merely "general supervision" but actual power over all aspects of the life of the "whole city." Despite their achievement of the right to vote and hold office during the second quarter of the nineteenth century, the mass of the city's male inhabitants were essentially powerless.

NOTES

1. For discussion of the electoral changes see Arthur W. MacMahon, *The Statutory Sources of New York City Government* (New York, 1923); Sidney I. Pomerantz, *New York: An American City, 1783–1803: A Study of Urban Life* (New York, 1938); Martha Lamb and Mrs. Burton Harrison, *History of the City of New York*, 3 vols. (New York, 1877–1896), vol. 3; and Robert Ludlow Fowler, "Constitutional and Legal History of New York," in James Grant Wilson, ed., *The Memorial History of the City of New York*, 5 vols. (New York, 1892–1893), vol. 3.

2. Edward Pessen, "The Social Configuration of the Antebellum City: An Historical and Theoretical Inquiry," *Journal of Urban History*, 2 (May 1976): 267–306; and Leonard P. Curry, "Urbanization and Urbanism in the Old South: A Comparative View," *Journal of Social History*, 40 (February 1974): 58.

3. Dahl, "Power, Pluralism and Democracy: A Modest Proposal," unpublished paper cited in Raymond E. Wolfinger, "Nondecisions and the Study of Local Politics," *American Political Science Review*, 65 (December 1971): 1080. For a sampling of scholarly definitions of power see Talcott Parsons, "Some Reflections on the Place of Power in Social Processes," in Harry Eckstein, ed., *Internal War* (New York, 1964), p. 57; Carl J. Friedrich, *Man and His Government: An Empirical Theory of Politics* (New York, 1963), pp. 199–200; Marvin E. Olson, "Power as a Social Process," in Olson, ed., *Power in Societies* (New York, 1970), p. 3; and James G. March, "The Power of Power," in David Easton, ed., *Varieties of Political Theory* (Englewood Cliffs, N.J., 1966), pp. 39–70.

4. Pessen, "Who Governed the Nation's Cities in the 'Era of the Common Man'?" *Political Science Quarterly*, 87 (Dec. 1972): 591–614.

5. In the interests of space, "Who Governed the Nation's Cities?" was documented by only a fragment of the author's "data bank."

6. There were twelve wards in 1826, seventeen by 1838, and eighteen by 1850.

7. For lists of the New York City rich that are based on the assessors' evaluations see Edward Pessen, "The Wealthiest New Yorkers of the Jacksonian Era: A New List," *New-York Historical Society Quarterly*, 54 (April 1970): 145–72. Assessments grossly undervalued real and above all personal property, but since they did so for most wealth holders, they are particularly useful as a clue to comparative wealth holdings.

8. After he completed his term as mayor in 1826, Philip Hone showed no interest in sitting on the council, where, in his words, "there is much to do and no pay." His refusal betrayed no disinterest in continued public service, for Hone now became more active than ever in an array of social service activities; see the manuscript diary of Hone in the New-York Historical Society, 1:240.

9. Hone diary, 2:27, 31, 66–67.

10. Brian J. Danforth, "The Influence of Socioeconomic Factors on Political Behavior: A Quantitative Look at New York City Merchants, 1828–1844" (New York University doctoral dissertation, 1974), 191–92.

11. One need not ask about design or purpose because the actual consequences of many measures are unanticipated by those who enact them. The fact that a bill enacted with the end in view, say, of promoting an influential private interest turns out instead to be harmful to that interest would hardly be proof of the political impotence of the interest in question.

12. See Stephan Thernstrom and Richard Sennett, eds., *Nineteenth-Century Cities: Essays in the New Urban History* (New Haven, 1969); and Leo F. Schnore, ed., *The New Urban History: Quantitative Explorations by American Historians* (Princeton, 1975).

13. For evidence on the conservative bias in the city's tax and tax assessment policies see *Minutes of the Common Council of the City of New York, 1784-1831* (New York, 1917), 8:437; *Report of the Special Committee of the Board of Supervisors Appointed to Examine the Assessment Rolls, and ascertain whether valuation in each Ward bears a just relation to the aggregate valuation in all the Wards* (New York City, Sept. 4, 1829); G. N. Bleecker, "Communication from the Comptroller on Subject of the Defective Manner of Assessing Personal Property in this City," Jan. 24, 1820, located in the New York City Municipal Archives and Records Center; and New York City Board of Assistant Aldermen, *Report of the Special Committee on the Subject of Equalizing Taxation* (New York, 1846), Doc. No. 18, p. 177. For the other issues see James F. Richardson, *The New York Police: Colonial Times to 1901* (New York, 1970); Carroll Smith-Rosenberg, *Religion and the Rise of the American City: The New York City Mission Movement 1812-1870* (Ithaca, 1971); John Duffy, *A History of Public Health in New York City (1625-1866)* (New York, 1968); *List of Real Estate Belonging to the Corporation of the City of New York* (New York, 1838); and *Proceedings of the Board of Aldermen, 1832-1833,* 4:416-18.

14. [William A. Brewer], *A Few Thoughts for Tax Payers and Voters* (New York, 1853), p. 74.

15. Frederick W. Frey, "Comments on Issues and Nonissues in the Study of Power," *American Political Science Review,* 65 (Dec. 1971): 1089-1101; Peter S. Bachrach and Morton S. Baratz, "Two Faces of Power," ibid., 56 (Dec. 1962): 947-52; and Wolfinger, "Nondecisions and the Study of Local Politics," pp. 1063-80.

16. Raymond A. Mohl, *Poverty in New York, 1783-1825* (New York, 1971).

17. See Jerome Mushkat, *Tammany: The Evolution of a Political Machine, 1789-1865* (Syracuse, 1971), 177-78; and Edward Pessen, *Riches, Class, and Power before the Civil War* (Lexington, Mass., 1973), p. 295.

18. Frank O. Gatell, "Money and Party in Jacksonian America: A Quantitative Look at New York City's Men of Quality," *Political Science Quarterly,* 87 (June 1967): 235-52. In determining who were the wealthiest men in the city, Gatell relied on the contemporary listings put out by Moses Y. Beach, the publisher of the *New York Sun.* For the unreliability of Beach's lists see Edward Pessen, "Moses Beach Revisited: A Critical Examination of His *Wealthy Citizens* Pamphlets," *Journal of American History,* 58 (Sept. 1971): 415-26.

19. Danforth, "The Influence of Socioeconomic Factors on Political Behavior," pp. 11, 180. Danforth's evidence is compelling.

20. Carl N. Degler, "The Locofocos: Urban 'Agrarians,' " *Journal of Economic History,* 16 (Sept. 1956): 322-33.

21. Edward Pessen, "The Working Men's Party Revisited," *Labor History,* 4 (Fall 1963): 203-26.

22. See Sam Bass Warner, Jr., *The Private City: Philadelphia in Three Periods of Its Growth* (Philadelphia, 1968); and the invaluable bibliographical discussion in Raymond A. Mohl, "The History of the American City," in William H. Cartwright and Richard L. Watson, eds., *The Reinterpretation of American History and Culture* (Washington, 1973), pp. 165-205.

23. For New York City see Pessen, *Riches, Class, and Power before the Civil War,* ch. 12; William W. Cutler, III, "Status, Values, and the Education of the Poor: The Trustees of the New York Public School Society, 1805-1853," *American Quarterly,* 24 (March 1972): 69-85; Raymond A. Mohl, "The Humane Society and Urban Reform in Early New York, 1787-1831," *New-York Historical Society Quarterly,* 54 (Jan. 1970): 30-52, and Mohl, *Poverty in New York;* Roy Lubove, "The New York Association for Improving the Condition of the Poor: The Formative Years," *New-York Historical Society*

Quarterly, 43 (July 1959): 307–27; Robert S. Pickett, *House of Refuge: Origins of Juvenile Reform in New York State, 1815–1857* (Syracuse, 1969); R. G. Vail, *Knickerbocker Birthday: A Sesquicentennial History of the New-York Historical Society, 1804–1954* (New York, 1954); Mary Bartlett Cowdrey, *The American Academy of Fine Arts and American Art-Union* (New York, 1953); see the manuscript diary of Philip Hone for regular references by an activist to his engagements in a variety of these organizations; and the following essays by M. J. Heale: "The New York Society for the Prevention of Pauperism, 1817–1823," *New-York Historical Society Quarterly,* 55 (April 1971): 153–76; "The Formative Years of the New York Prison Association, 1844–1862: A Case Study in Antebellum Reform," ibid., 59 (Oct. 1975): 320–47; and "From City Fathers to Social Critics: Humanitarianism and Government in New York City, 1790–1860," *Journal of American History,* 63 (June 1976): 21–46.

24. Tocqueville, *Democracy in America,* 2 vols. (New York, 1954), 2:115.

25. The quotations and generalizations cited in this section are drawn from the sources in note 23, the contemporary publications of the various associations, and the author's research in the private papers of their leaders.

26. For the radical ideology see Edward Pessen, *Most Uncommon Jacksonians: The Radical Leaders of the Early Labor Movement* (Albany, 1967), part 3.

27. Edward Pessen, "The Egalitarian Myth and the American Social Reality: Wealth, Mobility, and Equality in the 'Era of the Common Man,' " *American Historical Review,* 76 (Oct. 1971): 989–1034.

28. *Report of Committee of Trustees of the Free School Society on Distribution of the Common School Fund* (New York, 1825); and *An Address of the Trustees of the Public School Society in the City of New York to Their Fellow Citizens Respecting the Extension of Their Public Schools* (New York, 1828).

29. Warren F. Hewitt, "Samuel Breck and the Public School Law of 1834," *Pennsylvania History,* 1 (April 1934): 63–75.

30. James L. Crouthamel, *James Watson Webb: A Biography* (Middletown, Conn., 1969), is a good introduction to this issue.

31. Dolan, *The Immigrant Church: New York's Irish and German Catholics, 1815–1865* (Baltimore, 1975), p. 66.

32. Smith-Rosenberg, *Religion and the Rise of the American City,* p. 87.

33. Griffin, *Their Brothers' Keepers: Moral Stewardship in the United States, 1800–1865* (New Brunswick, N.J., 1960). On the conservative ideologies of leading Protestants see also Charles I. Foster, *An Errand of Mercy: The Evangelical United Front, 1790–1837* (Chapel Hill, 1960); Charles C. Cole, *The Social Ideas of the Northern Evangelists, 1826–1860* (New York, 1954); and John R. Bodo, *The Protestant Clergy and Public Issues* (Princeton, 1954).

34. For precisely such an investigation for antebellum Kingston, New York, see Stuart Blumin, "Church and Community: A Case Study of Lay Leadership in Nineteenth-Century America," *New York History,* 56 (October 1975): 393–408.

35. A number of "ethnocultural" interpretations of American political history, in drawing attention to the correlations between voters' denominational affiliations and their party preferences, reach conclusions about the depth of voters' religious convictions and the degree of influence of these convictions, on the basis of nothing better than superficial quantitative data on church memberships. See for example Richard Jensen, *The Winning of the Midwest: Social and Political Conflict, 1888–1896* (Chicago, 1971), and Paul J. Kleppner, *The Cross of Culture: A Social Analysis of Midwestern Politics, 1850–1900* (1970). For telling critiques of this approach see Richard L. McCormick, "Ethno-Cultural Interpretations of Nineteenth-Century American Voting Behavior," *Political Science Quarterly,* 89 (June 1974): 351–77; and J. Morgan

Kousser, "The 'New Political History': A Methodological Critique," *Reviews in American History*, 4 (March 1976): 1-14.
36. Pessen, "The Egalitarian Myth and the American Social Reality," 1022-24.
37. The assessors' notebooks are located in the New York City Municipal Archives and Records Center at 33 Park Row.
38. Manuscript diary of Philip Hone, 24:408.
39. Pessen, *Riches, Class, and Power before the Civil War*, passim.
40. *New York Daily Tribune*, July 9, 1845.
41. Griscom, *The Sanitary Condition of the Laboring Population of New York* (New York, 1845), and Gert H. Brieger, "Sanitary Reform in New York City: Stephen Smith and the Passage of the Metropolitan Health Bill," *Bulletin of the History of Medicine*, 40 (Sept.-Oct. 1966): 409.
42. Carl F. Kaestle, *The Evolution of an Urban School System: New York City, 1750-1850* (Cambridge, Mass., 1973), p. 189; David Grimsted, *Melodrama Unveiled: American Theatre and Culture, 1800-1850* (Chicago, 1968), pp. 55-56; Gerald N. Grob, *Mental Institutions in America: Social Policy to 1875* (New York, 1973); Charles E. Rosenberg, *The Cholera Years, The United States in 1832, 1849, and 1866* (Chicago, 1962), pp. 20, 29, 57; and John Duffy, *A History of Public Health in New York City*, pp. 409-16.
43. Pessen, *Riches, Class, and Power before the Civil War*, part 2.
44. Pessen, "Did Fortunes Rise and Fall Mercurially in Antebellum America? The Tale of Two Cities: Boston and New York," *Journal of Social History*, 4 (Summer 1971): 339-57.
45. See Danforth, "The Influence of Socioeconomic Factors on Political Behavior," pp. 98-103, for the "unrivalled" control exercised by New York City's merchant community over the city's banks, insurance companies, and marine insurance companies in the years 1828 to 1845. By checking the names of the officers and directors of these companies against the taxpayers' lists I asssembled from the assessment data, I discovered that very few of these businessmen were not among the upper 1 percent of wealth holders.
46. For a crystal-clear account of how this procedure was managed see James Sloane Gibbons, *The Banks of New York* (New York, 1858). Also informative on the power exercised by private bankers see Kenneth W. Porter, *John Jacob Astor, Businessman*, 2 vols. (Cambridge, Mass., 1931), 2: 955-56; Elva Tooker, *Nathan Trotter, Philadelphia Merchant, 1787-1853* (Cambridge, Mass., 1955); and Grant Morrison, "Isaac Bronson and the Search for System in American Capitalism, 1789-1838" (City University of New York doctoral dissertation, 1973).
47. Edward Pessen, "The Occupations of the Antebellum Rich: A Misleading Clue to the Sources and Extent of Their Wealth," *Historical Methods Newsletter*, 5 (March 1972): 49-52.
48. See John R. Commons and Associates, *History of Labour in the United States*, 4 vols., (New York, 1918), vol. 1; and Pessen, *Most Uncommon Jacksonians*, ch. 3.
49. Danforth, "The Influence of Socioeconomic Factors on Political Behavior," passim.
50. Heale, "From City Fathers to Social Critics," p. 24.

SELMA BERROL

3

WHO WENT TO SCHOOL IN
MID-NINETEENTH CENTURY NEW YORK?
AN ESSAY IN THE NEW URBAN HISTORY

For a very long time, American educational history was largely an inspirational history, cheerfully and complacently telling of growing enrollments, increased expenditures, and expanded courses of study. The heroes of this narrative were the professional educators, who fought and won the battle for the establishment and expansion of the tax-supported common school. The villains were the tight-fisted laymen and politicians, who held the purse strings and were never ready to spend the sums the schoolmen thought necessary.

This kind of simplistic history, although accurate enough in its larger outlines, told only part of the educational story because it represented solely the view from *inside* the educational establishment. Ellwood P. Cubberly's widely used *Public Education in the United States,* for example, described in profuse detail the growth of educational institutions and programs, but the children, who were the *raison d'efre* for the schools, do not appear on its pages.

In recent years, historians of education have tried to remove this "in-house" taint and bring the story of the schools into the mainstream of American social history. Beginning with Lawrence Cremin's *Transformation of the Schools,* a number of scholars have attempted to relate American educational developments to changing patterns in American life generally.[1] As part of the effort to broaden their work, some of these historians have tried to deal with the question of who went to school—the children of the poor? of the middle class? only of the rich? Their research has been in line with the increasing interest of historians generally in matters of social class and mobility.[2] Efforts to deal with these subjects, however, have been handicapped by an absence of primary sources. In New York City, for example, researchers had been unable to find any nineteenth-century school enrollment records and were forced to rely heavily on the works of William Bourne and Thomas Boese, both of whom held office in the educational bureaucracy of their day and, as a result, reported only the view from headquarters.

Recently, however, the register books of Grammar School 14, a boys school located on Twenty-seventh Street between Second and Third avenues near the boundary between the Eighteenth and Twenty-first wards, were discovered. Now, for the first time, it is possible to try to answer the question of whose children went to public school in mid-nineteenth century New York and to draw some conclusions about class, nativity, and education in one American city. That is what this essay will attempt to do.

In 1855, the year on which the study will focus, public education in New York City had been systematized and structured. A central Board of Education shared the responsibility for the schools with local boards, elected by the voters of the twenty-two wards into which the city was divided at that time. In every ward there were both primary and grammar schools. The former were for children at least five years old, and their function was to teach basic skills. In primary school a child was expected to learn simple arithmetic, a clear handwriting, and complete the first five reading books. There were no grade levels as we know them today; each youngster moved ahead at his own rate of learning. A student could be doing the simplest sums in arithmetic and at the same time be working on the most advanced reader. Because of this flexible and individualistic system and because the age of school entry varied a great deal, some children left primary school for grammar school at age eight and others at fifteen. Most made the change between ten and twelve, the usual age for mastery of the fifth reader.

The same system of continuous progress also existed in grammar school. Here, a child had to complete four additional readers and build on the rudimentary writing and arithmetical skills learned earlier. If he remained long enough, he would also be taught history, geography, and mathematics. The full grammar school course included commercial subjects as well. The mid-nineteenth-century New York City grammar school, it would appear, was a multipurpose secondary school. For most youngsters, it provided reinforcement and expansion of the minimal skills they had learned in primary school. For some it was vocational, and for a very small number it was preparatory to higher education.[3]

The abundance of material in the register books of Grammar School 14 (over twelve thousand names, covering the years 1835 to 1866, complete with address, subjects studied, age upon entry, and father's name and occupation) can be misleading. Even with so much historical raw material available, this study must be a limited one, and the conclusions can only be tentative. What the data can tell us is who among the boys aged eight to fifteen living in the Eighteenth and Twenty-first wards of New York City in the middle of the nineteenth century attended this particular grammar school. In the absence of other school records, we cannot determine who went to primary (surely a much larger number), who went to other grammar schools, public or private, or whether the students at Grammar School 14 were typical of the boys of this age who went beyond primary school in the city as a whole.[4]

Furthermore, although they were of great interest, the records alone could not even provide a meaningful answer to the question of who went to *this* school. To find that most of the boys in the school were the sons of skilled workers, for example, would be interesting; but the real significance comes from knowing what proportion of the eligible sons of skilled workers they were, especially when compared with the proportions in which other groups were represented. There might be only a few sons of unskilled workers in school, for example, but their small number might represent a larger proportion of those eligible. The data in the register books, therefore, were valuable only when compared with the data available for the total eligible population. The existence of the New York State census for 1855 made it possible to make exactly such a comparison.

From this enumeration, it appears that the Eighteenth and Twenty-first wards, which together encompassed the areas between Fourteenth and Fortieth streets from Sixth Avenue to the East River and contained seventy-one thousand inhabitants, was quite a prosperous district.[5] The area west of Third Avenue contained mostly single family dwellings large enough to house a big family and occupy several servants. The families who lived on these blocks were headed by managers, entrepreneurs, professionals of various kinds (brokers, bankers, doctors, and lawyers) as well as a number of gentlemen who told the census taker that they did not need to work at all.

The other districts of the two wards contained multiple dwellings, inhabited mostly by middle-class families, where the head of the household was likely to be a skilled worker, a government employee, a clerk, or a salesman. Only the easternmost area, from First Avenue to the East River, contained many low-income families, who, although poor, were not destitute. They were rather the laboring poor, working as cartmen, drovers, seamstresses, and servants. On these blocks, too, lived the few residents who told the census taker they were without jobs of any kind.[6] The small number of unemployed was probably due to the abundance of work available in the district. Although, as one would expect, the westerly élite neighborhoods were entirely residential, the remainder of the two wards contained a great variety of small-scale processing and manufacturing plants. Both the census and the school records make it clear that the people of the area took full advantage of the available opportunities. Parental occupations closely matched existing enterprises. Since there were so many slaughterhouses, a great many men were butchers; because the Empire Stone Dressing Plant covered the entire area from Twenty-eighth to Thirtieth streets and from First Avenue to the river, there were many stonecutters; because there were a number of pianoforte factories on Fourth Avenue, there were many piano workers living in the Eighteenth and Twenty-first wards.[7]

This happy marriage between workers and jobs was not fortuitous. The data showed that most of the inhabitants had moved into the area within the previous decade, probably attracted by increasing employment opportunities. Until 1846, the district had not had enough people to be organized as a ward; seven years later, however, there were so many people that the Eighteenth Ward had to be divided, and the Twenty-first was formed. Although most of the residents had not been born in the area, almost all had previously lived elsewhere in New York City and thus were aware of the developments taking place north of Fourteenth Street. Of the heads of households, 42 percent had been born somewhere in the Empire City, and many of the rest (57.9 percent), although they had not been born in New York, had lived there for some time. Most of this latter group was foreign born, largely from Ireland, Germany, and England; but a sizable number had started life in other states (mostly in New England) and another significant segment had moved in from various New York counties.[8]

The marshal's manuscript schedule for the Eighteenth and Twenty-first wards showed that in 1855 this comfortable and heterogeneous population included 3,845 boys aged eight to fifteen. To carry out this study, the name of each eligible boy was noted, and—except for the youths who were self-supporting—that of his parent or guardian. Parental occupation, nativity, and length of residence in New York City were also listed, except for the boys who lived alone. For the latter, the boys' own occupation, nativity, and length of residence were used. The school records were then searched in order to see which of the boys listed in the census were registered at the school any time in 1855.

Only 580 or 15 percent of the eligible boys were enrolled in Grammar School 14 in 1855. This small proportion can be explained in a number of ways. First of all, there was no compulsory education law, nor were there any child labor laws. As a result, 4.2 percent of the potential students were self-supporting; and an unknown number, for whom no occupation was listed because they lived with their families, were undoubtedly also employed. Secondly, because they had not attained the reading level required to move on to the next class, others were still attending primary school. Still others were enrolled in private schools. In addition, zoning was unknown, and residents were free to chose a school anywhere in the city. Although most parents probably chose a neighborhood school for their children, Grammar School 14 certainly did not have a monopoly on the qualified students in the area. The Eighteenth and Twenty-first wards had two other educational institutions containing primary and grammar divisions for both sexes. One of these was at Twentieth Street between First and Second avenues and the other, newly completed, was located at Thirty-seventh Street between Second and Third avenues.[9]

Even if the latter school had not been built, however, it does not seem that Grammar School 14 could have accommodated more students than it already had. The school occupied a lot of 100 feet by 100 feet, but the building itself was only 42 feet wide by 99 feet deep. It was three stories high and contained four long, narrow classrooms per floor. Considering that these relatively small quarters were shared with two sizable primary schools and a small grammar school for girls, it is hard to see how even 580 grammar school boys were accommodated.[10]

The crowding may help to explain why—in spite of a statement in an 1855 report by the superintendent of schools that the public schools under his jurisdiction were "extensively attended by the children of our most respectable citizens"—the sons of gentlemen, merchants, managers, and professionals were not enrolled in this grammar school in substantial numbers.[11] With their greater resources, upper-class parents would not normally send their sons to an overcrowded public school.

It comes as no surprise, therefore, to see that there were no young gentlemen at all in Grammar School 14 in 1855, although they constituted 2 percent of the total eligible population. (See Table 1.) Merchants' sons comprised only 0.5 percent of the students registered, although they made up 7.6 percent of those eligible. The proportion of sons from the professional and managerial groups who were in school (4.4 percent) was closer to the incidence of this group in the population (5.5 percent); but on the whole, the sons of the gentry were only a small minority in the school and

TABLE 1
PERCENTAGE OF ELIGIBLE BOYS IN GRAMMAR SCHOOL 14 IN 1855 (CLASSIFIED BY PARENTAL OCCUPATION)

Occupation	Eligible Population		School Population	
Gentlemen	2.0		0	
Merchants	7.6		0.5	
Professionals and Managers	5.5		4.4	
Total upper-class		15.1		4.9
Skilled workers	31.0		41.7	
Government employees, including military	1.9		1.5	
Clerical	2.3		1.8	
Sales	5.6		8.6	
Total middle-class		40.8		53.6
Unskilled workers	14.8		14.1	
Employed widows	5.2		3.6	
Unemployed widows	7.4		11.5	
Miscellaneous*	8.0		10.8	
No occupation	2.7		0	
Service	1.8		1.5	
Employed (boys)	4.2		0	
Total lower-class		44.1		41.5
Total	100.00		100.00	

*Includes workers on the New York and Harlem Railroad, deckhands on ferries, seamen, and omnibus drivers.
Source: *New York State Census,* 1855, and register books of Grammar School 14, New York City.

were quite underrepresented in proportion to their numbers in the eligible population. Taken together, the sons of these well-to-do fathers constituted about 15 percent of the eligible population but only 5 percent of the school population.

The sons of middle-class fathers (skilled workers, government employees, clerks, and sales persons), on the other hand, constituted 53.6 percent of the boys registered in Grammar School 14, although they comprised only 40.8 percent of the eligible population. Government employees' sons were 1.9 percent of the eligibles and 1.5 percent of those in school. Those whose fathers were clerical workers also approximated their proportion in the eligible population (1.8 percent to 2.3 percent). The sons of skilled workers, however, were *overrepresented* in the school population (41.7 percent to 31 percent), as were those whose fathers were salesmen (8.6 percent to 5.6 percent); the boys from these two groups mainly gave Grammar School 14 its distinctly middle-class profile.[12]

The remainder of the students were the sons of parents in less remunerative and lower status occupations. They comprised 44.1 percent of the eligible population and 41.5 percent of the school population and were therefore represented in reasonable proportion to their incidence in the general population. Of these, 14.1 percent were the children of unskilled workers, closely approximating their proportion, 14.8 percent, in the eligible population. Another 10.8 percent were the sons of parents who performed a miscellany of jobs: flagmen on the railroads, deckhands on the ferries, seamen on ocean-going cargo ships, and drivers on omnibuses. Parents like these constituted 8.0 percent of the eligible population. Only 1.5 percent of the students were the sons of servants, which was similar to the incidence of this group in the population (1.8 percent). A surprisingly large number of parents with eligible sons were widows. The sons of employed widows, who constituted 5.2 percent of those eligible, were somewhat underrepresented in Grammar School 14, comprising only 3.6 percent of the population. On the other hand, the sons of unemployed widows, who made up 7.4 percent of the eligibles, were overrepresented and constituted 11.5 percent of all the students in school. Families headed by an unemployed male, who constituted 2.7 percent of the eligible population, sent no sons to Grammar School 14. The names of the 4.2 percent of the eligible boys who were employed were, of course, also missing from the register books.

From all of the above, it seems clear that in these two wards at least, the sons of the middle and working classes (especially the former) were the mainstay of the public schools. The distribution at Grammar School 14 was similar to the pattern which had existed in the New York common schools for many years. An analysis of the occupations of parents of children in New York City charity and pay schools in 1796 (before the city had a public school system) showed that 50 percent of the students were from middle-class homes and 14 percent were from lower-class families.[13]

Forty-four years later, Theodore Sedgewick, a spokesman for the publicly funded but privately controlled Public School Society, said that a fifth of the sixteen thousand students in the society's schools were the children of laborers and widows, and that most of the others were from homes of artisans—shoemakers, cabinet makers, and the like. Sedgewick concluded, "Of clergymen's sons there are but 13; of doctor's 44; lawyers 25 and the sons of gentlemen figure in the last only to the amount of 26."[14]

It is not difficult to see why the sons of the middle class and especially those of skilled workers were overrepresented in the school population. Although they could not afford to pay tuition, they *could* afford to do without the income their boy might earn. Many lower-class parents were also willing to do this, although for them, of course, the sacrifice was much greater. Because of this, while lower-class boys were represented at Grammar School 14 in accord with their numbers in the eligible population, the sons of skilled workers were enrolled in a greater proportion.

It is somewhat more difficult to know why the sons of unemployed widows were so overrepresented in the school population, especially when those whose mothers were employed were less well represented. In a society that provided no aid to dependent children or public assistance of any kind, why did so many widows allow a potential breadwinner to attend school instead of earning money? Unlike today, there were many jobs available for young, untrained boys. Of the males aged eight to fifteen in wards Eighteen and Twenty-one, 4.2 percent were supporting themselves as servants, clerks, or apprentices in a variety of trades, and it is reasonable to assume that most of the widows' sons could have found similar jobs.

The census data, however, give some clues to this puzzle. What distinguished an employed widow from one who did not work was the absence of children old enough to hold a reasonably well paid job. When a woman had older sons able to earn enough money, her younger ones attended school. When all of her children were in their early teens or younger, she worked as a seamstress, washerwoman, or cleaner, and her sons were not as likely to be enrolled at Grammar School 14. Although the census did not list an occupation for them, they were probably doing whatever they could to earn some much-needed income for their family.

The fact that older siblings in fatherless working-class families would be willing to support a younger brother through grammar school is somewhat surprising and contradicts some of the conventional wisdom about the nineteenth-century laboring poor. At least some members of this class apparently saw formal schooling as a positive good and were willing to make considerable sacrifices in order to have a younger member of the family receive an extended education.

Judging from the subjects studied in Grammar School 14, the boy who attended and did well might reasonably expect to obtain a higher status occupation than the one held by his father or older brother. In addition to algebra, drawing, astronomy, and geography, which would not have much vocational value, the boys were taught a great deal of arithmetic, especially business arithmetic and bookkeeping, which would provide training for the clerical opportunities provided by the expanding commercial life of New York City. Other evidence that the grammar school curriculum was designed to prepare the boys for jobs was the emphasis on handwriting (essential for a clerk in the era before typewriters), grammar, etymology, and composition, all of which might help a young man to obtain a white-collar position. Whether the investment (if that is really how it was seen) did indeed result in upward mobility will be the subject of a different investigation.[15]

The foregoing analysis indicated that parental occupation and consequent socioeconomic status influenced public school enrollment in mid-nineteenth century New York City but does not appear to have been the dominant factor. Although the boys from the wealthiest families in the area did not attend Grammar School 14 and although the sons of skilled workers and unemployed widows were present in unusually large numbers, the children of other socioeconomic groups were generally represented in accord with their proportions in the eligible population. Other factors, therefore, may have been more influential.

What of parental nativity? Who was more likely to go to grammar school, the son of an American-born or foreign-born father? As Table 2 shows, it appears to be the former. Boys whose fathers had been born abroad constituted 64.3 percent of the eligible population but were only 57.1 percent of the students enrolled. The sons of native-born fathers, on the other hand, comprised only 35.4 percent of the eligible population but made up 42.6 percent of those in school. These figures, however, mask the real situation. Boys whose fathers had been born in Ireland, Germany, England, and Scotland attended Grammar School 14 in accord with their incidence in the eligible population. Only the sons of men born in France, Poland, Italy, and Switzerland were underrepresented, and it was really the absence of boys from these groups that accounted for the apparent underenrollment of sons of foreign-born fathers.

Although their small number makes any explanation hazardous, several reasons could account for the scarcity of boys from French, Italian, Polish, or Swiss families at Grammar School 14. The French were generally upper-class, and an excellent French private school existed in New York. The

TABLE 2
PERCENTAGE OF ELIGIBLE BOYS IN GRAMMAR SCHOOL 14 IN 1855 CLASSIFIED BY PARENTAL NATIVITY

Nativity	Eligible Population	School Population
Ireland	41.8	40.8
Germany	10.3	8.1
England	6.7	5.8
Other foreign-born	5.5	2.4
New York City	15.7	32.5
New York State	9.6	6.2
Other states	10.1	3.9
Totals*	99.7	99.7

*Rounded to nearest decimal.
Source: *New York State Census,* 1855, and Register Books of Grammar School 14, New York City.

families from Poland were almost all Jews, and although the East European Jews who came to New York later in the century made full use of the free public schools, this earlier group, perhaps because the fathers were all self-employed craftsmen able to give their sons "on the job" training," did not do so. The few Italian fathers with sons eligible to attend were all barbers, and they, like the Polish Jews, may have preferred to educate their sons in the shop. The Swiss-born fathers were almost uniformly employed in the pianoforte factories that lined Fourth Avenue, and since they were highly skilled and well paid, they may have chosen a private, sectarian school for their sons.

More important than the underrepresentation of the smaller groups is the fact that sons of Irish-, German-, and English-born fathers were enrolled in accord with their proportion in the eligible population. Most of these men had come from areas of Europe where children of the underprivileged classes were not expected to go to any kind of school for very long. As Robert Ernst points out, the widespread illiteracy of the vast majority of the Irish who came to New York prior to 1850 made it almost impossible to establish an Irish press, and until the arrival of the "Forty-eighters" the educated German community in the city was too small to sustain any intellectual life. "America letters" have been credited with stimulating "emigration fever" from various regions in Europe, but these letters were often written by a paid scribe in the United States and read to all comers by one of the few literate men in the village. In view of the fact that many of the foreign-born parents of boys eligible to attend grammar school had little previous experience with free nonsectarian education, especially on the secondary level, it is somewhat surprising to see that their sons were well represented at Grammar School 14. [16]

Unfamiliarity with formal education, however, was probably not as powerful an influence on the foreign-born parents of the Eighteenth and Twenty-first wards as it would have been in the Sixth or Tenth wards, areas which contained most of the newly arrived and most impoverished immigrants. The district served by Grammar School 14 was at least the second place of residence for most of the parents who had been born abroad, and therefore they were neither quite so poor nor uninformed as the more recent arrivals who lived downtown. As a result, although they had not been born in New York, they could have become aware of the opportunities the city offered to those who were educated. While nineteenth-century society certainly did not stress educational credentials to the extent that we have done in the twentieth century, even in the 1850s a grammar school diploma could pave the way to some social and economic improvement, and many of the foreign-born parents may have understood this and acted accordingly. This awareness and the absence of a parochial grammar school in the area, for example, probably explained why even Irish parents, although usually considered to be among the poorest of immigrants, sent their children to Grammar School 14 in proportion to their incidence in the eligible population.

As was true for those born abroad, a closer look at the various categories of native-born parents also reveals important differences obscured by the overall percentages. As Table 2 shows, only the sons of New York City–born fathers were overrepresented at Grammar School 14. Boys whose fathers were born elsewhere in New York State or in another state were surprisingly underrepresented. These native-born parents must surely have been aware of the opportunities New York City presented to an educated man. And since they were mostly from the northeast, where some kind of common school had existed in most communities for a good part of the nineteenth century, they were also familiar with the uses and value of formal education. Why, then, were their sons underrepresented? Because these fathers were affluent enough to send their boys to private school. Almost a third of the native-born fathers whose birthplace was other than New York City were merchants, professionals, managers, or gentlemen. No other group was so well represented among those with upper-class occupations.

By contrast, the great majority of New York City–born parents were in middle-class occupations and sent their sons to public school because they were less able to pay tuition. In addition, many fathers in this group may have had direct experience with the schools in their native city. Free education of some sort had been a fact in New York since 1805, and a truly public school system had been in operation since 1842. Although it is impossible to know how many of the New York City-born parents who now had sons eligible to enroll at Grammar School 14 had attended public school in their own childhood, it *is* possible to say that the opportunity to attend had existed in New York City for several generations and that as a result, this group of parents was familiar with the idea of free public schooling. Also, longer residence meant more knowledge of the economy and the opportunities which existed in the city. For these reasons, the native New York parent might have seen ample reason to invest in extended schooling for his sons.

From this analysis it appears that length of residence in the city, not parental nativity per se, was an important influence on public school enrollment in mid-nineteenth century New York. It is true that the sons of native-born New Yorkers were very much overrepresented at Grammar School 14, but most of the boys from foreign-born families were not underrepresented. It would seem that New York–born fathers, having lived in the city the longest, were most aware of the value of formal schooling; but many of their foreign-born peers apparently had been residents long enough to adopt a similar attitude.

Attendance at a school and completion of the course of study are often very different matters. Did most of the boys who were enrolled at Grammar School 14 in 1855 remain to graduate? Was their success or the lack of it related to their fathers' occupational status or place of birth? To begin with, only 68 of the 580 boys who enrolled in 1855 actually graduated. The number of years they spent at the school before receiving their diploma varied with their previous preparation, but most of them attended from one to three years. The other 512 dropped out at various points in their grammar school career, many in their first year.

Although the small number of graduates makes it difficult to draw any firm conclusions, it does appear that successful completion of grammar school was related to parental socioeconomic status. While boys from upper-class homes comprised only 5 percent of the population enrolled in 1855, they were 11 percent of those who graduated. The sons of middle-class fathers constituted 53.6 percent of the boys who were registered but were 66 percent of those who graduated. Boys whose fathers were in lower-class occupations made up 41 percent of the students in 1855, but were only 23 percent of those who graduated. Adequate parental income, it would appear, made it more likely that a boy would earn a grammar school diploma.

Parental nativity was also a factor. Although 57.1 percent of the boys enrolled in 1855 came from foreign-born parents, only 43 percent of the graduates were from such backgrounds. Of the students who were registered in 1855, 42.6 percent were the sons of native born fathers; but 57 percent of those who graduated were in this position. The students with Irish-born fathers, who had made up 40.8 percent of the enrollment, constituted only 25 percent of the graduates, while those who were second-generation New Yorkers, originally 32.5 percent of the school population, were 41 percent of the graduates. Boys whose fathers were born elsewhere in New York State, originally only 6.2 percent of those enrolled, were 16 percent of those who graduated. None of the small (3.9 percent) group of boys whose fathers originated in other parts of the United States finished the course of study at Grammar School 14, and the sons of foreign-born parents whose birthplace was other than Ireland appeared in the graduating class in roughly the same proportion they had been in the school population (18 percent enrolled to 16 percent graduated).

From these figures, it would seem that parental nativity and socio-economic status had more effect on school completion than on enrollment. In the latter instance, as we have seen, it was mostly the sons of skilled workers and fathers who were born in New York City that were overrepresented at Grammar School 14. In terms of school completion, however, *all* of the sons of native-born fathers were overrepresented, as were those from upper- and middle-class homes. Boys from lower-class families and those whose fathers had been born in Ireland, on the other hand, while enrolled at Grammar School 14 in proportion to their incidence in the eligible population, were very much underrepresented among the graduates. The small sample makes generalization difficult, but it does seem that low family income or an Irish background, while not preventing a boy from beginning grammar school, did interfere with completion.

Only eleven of the graduates were able and ambitious enough to be admitted to the highly selective Free Academy, the sole free high school in the city at that time. The nativity and socioeconomic status of this group (as judged by place of parental birth and occupation) was not very different from the population of the school as a whole, or that of the graduates who did not go on to the Free Academy. Six of their parents were born in New York City, one in Ireland, one in Germany, two in England, and one in Westchester County. Nine came from middle-class families. They were the sons of skilled workers, retail proprietors, and a real estate agent. Two of the boys, however, were the sons of unemployed widows. Since, as discussed earlier, it must have been difficult enough for a widow to support a son through grammar school, it is quite surprising to note that some of these boys managed to go on to high school.

It is also interesting to see that none of the eight merchants' or professionals' sons who attended in 1855 and who remained to graduate were admitted to the Free Academy. Perhaps they were all dullards (although their records indicate that they passed all the required subjects within a reasonable period of time); it is more likely that their fathers could afford to send them to a private academy and that for this reason, they did not even apply.[17]

As the previous pages have shown, if the records of Grammar School 14 are representative of the city as a whole, most boys in mid-nineteenth century New York probably did not go to public grammar school at all. They were most likely to go if their fathers were skilled workers and had been born in New York City. If, in addition, they were bright enough, boys from such homes were also very likely to be among the small group of graduates and the even smaller number of students who went on to the Free Academy. In short, children who were at least second-generation New Yorkers and whose fathers had a trade were most likely to make full use of the city's free education system.

In many respects, these conclusions were to be expected. Estimates of New York City wage scales at mid century indicate that skilled workers were paid twice as much as those who were unskilled. They were, therefore, better able to keep their sons off the labor market and send them to school instead. In addition, probably because English was their parents' native tongue, most of the boys whose fathers were born in New York City entered Grammar School at a higher reading level than did those who came from non-English-speaking homes. Not for the last time in urban educational history, family background strongly influenced school achievement. As is often the case, it is likely that boys who did well were more interested in completing school and that their parents were more interested in making the financial sacrifice. Because they could better afford additional schooling and because their boys could make good use of it, it is not surprising to see that the sons of skilled workers and native-born New Yorkers were overrepresented at Grammar School 14.

What is surprising, however, is to see that boys from lower-class families and those with foreign-born fathers were represented at the school in proportion to their incidence in the eligible population. In view of the fact that in 1855 New York City parents were not compelled to send their sons to *any* school, let alone grammar school, the substantial representation of boys from low-income and foreign-born homes seems quite remarkable and indicates a positive attitude toward formal education not usually attributed to these groups. How can this be explained?

First of all, recent studies indicate that even in the absence of compulsory education laws, nineteenth-century parents, everywhere in the United States, were willing to send their children to school. According to a leading historian of education, David Tyack, there was "a broad consensus on the value of schooling, [and] levels of literacy and school attendance were very high in the United States [even] before the common school revival of the 1840's and 1850's." While they shared in the consensus, New York City parents had some special reasons to hold formal education in high regard, and these additional factors explain why so many of the sons of laborers and the foreign-born were enrolled at Grammar School 14.[18]

New York at mid century was a dynamic and expanding commercial city, full of opportunities for those with clerical skills of any kind. Schooling could lead to employment in the flourishing countinghouses and mercantile establishments located in the city center, and many blue-collar parents may have wanted such white-collar positions for their sons. Judging from the makeup of the student body and the subjects taught, many of the boys at Grammar School 14 were there to learn skills that would enable them to enter the working world at a level higher than that of their fathers. While it is undoubtedly true that many routes to upward mobility existed in the Empire City, formal schooling was certainly one of them, and the realization of this fact may have impelled many low-income parents, especially if they had lived in New York for some time, to send their sons to schools like Grammar School 14.

The register books of the school make it clear that the assumed link between education and upward social mobility, so much a part of our social fabric today, existed in the nineteenth century as well. Because they contain information about the students and important data on their parents, the records of Grammar School 14 allow us to gain some insight into who went to school in nineteenth-century New York City and to understand their motivations for doing so. For these reasons, they provide a valuable window on the urban past.

NOTES

*   I would like to acknowledge the assistance of a grant from the Baruch College Scholar Assistance Fund which made it possible to duplicate the fragile register books of Grammar School 14. I also wish to thank my husband, Edward Berrol, for his valuable guidance on the statistical portions of this study.

1.   In addition to Cremin's seminal work, see Michael Katz, *The Irony of Early School Reform* (Cambridge: Harvard University Press, 1968); Colin Greer, *The Great School Legend* (New York: Basic Books, 1972); Marvin Lazerson, *Origins of the Urban School* (Cambridge: Harvard University Press, 1971); Carl Kaestle, *The Evolution of an Urban School System* (Cambridge: Harvard University Press, 1973); Stanley K. Schultz, *The Culture Factory* (New York: Oxford University Press, 1973); David Tyack, *The One Best System* (Cambridge: Harvard University Press, 1974).

2.   Stephan Thernstrom's *Poverty and Progress* (Cambridge: Harvard University Press, 1964) and *The Other Bostonians* (Cambridge: Harvard University Press, 1973) pioneered "the new urban history." He has been joined by many other historians, including Howard Chudacoff, who wrote *Mobile Americans* (New York: Oxford University Press, 1972) and Thomas Kessner, *The Golden Door: Italian and Jewish Immigrant Mobility in New York City, 1880-1915* (New York: Oxford University Press, 1977).

3.   Kaestle, *Evolution of an Urban School System,* p. 172; Diane Ravitch, *The Great School Wars* (New York: Basic Books, 1974), pp. 13, 85; Thomas Boese, *Public Education in the City of New York* (New York: Harper Bros., 1869), p. 132.

4.   Addresses are available only for boys who registered after 1853, when the demise of the Public School Society brought Grammar School 14 under the jurisdiction of the Board of Education.

5.   New York State, *Census of the State of New York, 1855* (Albany, 1857), summary volume, 38. Assuming that the positions held by the parents of the boys eligible to attend grammar school were representative of the occupations

held by the breadwinners of the wards as a whole (not unreasonable in view of the fact that families with eligible boys constituted a third of the 11,535 families in the wards), it would appear that the people of these two wards were more prosperous than the population of the city in general. Only 14.8 percent of the heads of families with eligible boys in wards Eighteen and Twenty-one were unskilled workers, while the citywide proportion was 27 percent. Only 31 percent of the fathers of eligible sons in these wards were skilled workers; citywide, 41 percent were. It would seem that the gentlemen, merchants, professionals, and white-collar workers who chose to live in these uptown districts gave the area a more prosperous mien than that of the city as a whole. Citywide figures are from Kaestle, *Evolution of an Urban School System*, 102-3.

6. *Census of the State of New York, 1855.* Although the manuscript census schedule does not give addresses, it *is* divided by election districts. The New York County Clerk's office (where the census is stored) has prepared a guide which gives the geographic boundaries of each election district. Thanks to this helpful device, it was possible to see that the westerly first election district of each ward was home to men of property and standing. The census showed their upper-class occupations, the high value of their homes, and their many servants.

7. John F. Harrison, *Map of the City of New York Extending Northward to Fiftieth Street* (New York: M. Dripps, 1851); in the Stokes Collection of the New York Public Library. Also, William Perris (ed.) *Maps of the City of New York,* vol. 6 (1854), at the New York Historical Society. The latter were prepared for fire insurance purposes and show every building standing on every block of the area they cover. The Perris maps give visual reinforcement to the economic summaries that follow the enumeration of population for each election district in the census.

8. In 1855, New York City consisted of Manhattan alone. *Census of the State of New York, 1855.* Dates for the organization of the two wards appear on the first page of the volume pertaining to that ward. Data on nativity appears in the summary volume for the entire census, pp. 112-18.

9. Boese, *Public Education,* p. 138; New York City, Board of Education, *Annual Report,* 1855, p. 90.

10. Board of Education, *Report,* 1855, pp. 5-6.

11. Ibid., p. 82.

12. Historians studying social mobility have difficulty assigning class status to occupations. Is a clerk middle-class because he works with his head more than his hands? Or is he really part of the working class because his income is low? Should the determinant of class be income? Prestige? I have tried to incorporate what seemed to me to be most valid in the work done by the scholars noted above, and I have also consulted the scale developed by Professor Donald J. Treiman of the Center for Policy Research of Columbia University (Donald J. Treiman, "Standard International Occupational Prestige Scale for Historical Data," unpublished manuscript, 1972). After all this, I have placed skilled workers in the middle class because they earned twice as much as unskilled workers did. (See Carol Pernicone, "The Bloody Old Sixth," unpublished Ph.D. dissertation, Dept. of History, University of Rochester, 1973, pp. 99, 101; George Rogers Taylor, "The Beginnings of Mass Transportation in Urban America," *Smithsonian Journal of History,* 1 [Summer, 1966] : 48.) Also, they resided in the middle portion of the two wards, neither in the most westerly élite district nor on the most easterly blocks, which also contained the slaughterhouses, gas works, and quarries, where the poorest residents lived. Finally, most of them were truly craftsmen and had status and income far above the cartmen, drovers, and laborers, whom I have placed among the unskilled. I have also placed clerks in the middle class because they needed some education to hold such a position, and it seemed to me that in a society

in which most men did not receive such an education (as this paper shows), having the skills necessary for clerking gave the individual middle-class status. I have also placed government employees in this class, although their occupations ranged from constable to customshouse official. It is clear that although they all had a governmental agency as their employer, their income and status must have varied a good deal. But what *is* the class status of a policeman even today? Or that of the inspector who checks one's luggage at Kennedy Airport? Finding it impossible to answer these questions even for the present, and aware that some of them would be in the wrong category, I nonetheless placed all the government employees of 1855 into the middle class.

13. Kaestle, *Evolution of an Urban School System*, p. 54. Kaestle also found that 26 percent of the students were from upper-class homes, a sharp difference from the 5 percent enrolled at Grammar School 14 in 1855. The explanation is his inclusion of *pay* schools in his summary.

14. William O. Bourne, *History of the Public School System* (New York: William Wood, 1870), p. 234. I am indebted to Professor William Cutler of Temple University for bringing Sedgewick's statement to my attention.

15. Taylor, "Beginnings of Mass Transportation," p. 38.

16. Robert Ernst, *Immigrant Life in New York City* (Port Washington, N.Y.: Ira J. Friedman, 1949), pp. 150, 145; Philip Taylor, *The Distant Magnet* (New York: Harper and Row, 1971), pp. 86–88. The occupations of the great majority of immigrants who arrived at the port of New York between 1820 and 1860 provide additional evidence regarding the low educational level of most foreign-born fathers. Of the 2,480,822 passengers who gave their occupations, only 29,400 were in professions which would require some formal education. See Friedrich Kapp, *Immigration and the Commissioners of Emigration of the State of New York* (New York: Douglas Taylor, 1870), p. 229.

17. The absence of any upper-class boys from the group of Grammar School 14 graduates who went to the Free Academy might not have been the usual pattern. When Carl Kaestle tabulated the occupations of parents with sons in the Academy for the years 1849–1853, he found that over 15 percent were merchants or professionals—categories I have labeled upper-class (Kaestle, *Evolution of an Urban School System*, p. 107). It is likely that some of the sons of well-to-do fathers, although they attended a private grammar school, utilized the Free Academy as their preparatory school. This might explain why I found no upper-class graduates from Grammar School 14 going to the Academy and why Kaestle, who was not tracing boys from grammar school, found many.

18. Tyack, *One Best System*, p. 66.

DONALD SIMON

4

GREEN-WOOD CEMETERY AND THE AMERICAN PARK MOVEMENT

It was in Chicago, on July 12, 1893, that Frederick Jackson Turner delivered a paper before the American Historical Association and set off a debate that continues to this day. Entitled "The Significance of the Frontier in American History," Turner's paper asserted that the source of American development was to be explained by the "existence of an area of free land, its continuous recession, and the advance of American settlement westward."[1] This idea, generally known as the "frontier hypothesis," claims that the institutions of the United States owe their development in a significant measure to a constant interplay of man and his surroundings. Although much of what Turner said has been criticized and modified, he made a major contribution in emphasizing environmentalism as a factor in American development.

It is interesting that Turner delivered his seminal paper in Chicago, for it was in that very city at the same time that the World's Columbian Exposition was delighting visitors with demonstrations of technological and industrial innovations. It may well be one of the ironies of history that Turner drew attention to the American environment at a time when many Americans were accepting the notion that man had tamed nature. To realize how important this new belief was, one need but recall that nature had been a great impediment to American development. Vast distances, steep mountains, apparently endless forests and prairies all restricted movement and commerce. All of this forced Americans to be respectful of nature.

Born of this respect for nature there emerged a feeling that those who did battle with the environment and triumphed were doing God's work.

This so-called agrarian myth maintained that purity and virtue were to be found on the farm. Henry Nash Smith refers to this when he notes that "the image of an agricultural paradise . . . embodying group memories of an earlier, a simpler and, it was believed, a happier state of society long survived as a force in American thought and politics."[2]

Early evidence of this view is seen in the attitudes of the average American of the late eighteenth and early nineteenth century, who found little to admire in cities. George Washington's secretary of the treasury, Alexander Hamilton, was the exception, in that he saw virtue in manufacturing and cities. Generally, however, cities were feared, condemned, and opposed. At a time when few Americans anticipated or wanted the growth of larger cities in the nation, little attention was directed toward eradicating urban ills such as the lack of sanitation, inadequate water supply, and poor housing, conditions of urban life that early became evident. In an era before commerce and industry drew vast numbers of people to the cities, when open space was easily attainable, and at a time when rivers and ponds were still unpolluted, people could find places of recreation near at hand. Understandably, there was little demand for a conscious park-recreation movement.

The earliest public parks in America were not for recreation. They were public reserves of land that served as common pasturage, military parade grounds, or city ornament. The first park was Boston's famous Common. This ground, used for pasturing the town's cows and for a drill ground, remained America's only "public park" until 1682, when William Penn, "foreseeing the rapid growth of his city, ordered five squares laid off and set aside for the permanent use of its people."[3] Boston and Philadelphia were joined by Newport in 1713 when it opened a common, but it was not until 1733, when the Corporation of New York leased land on lower Broadway and then laid it out as a bowling green, that there was a true park in the modern sense. The history of America's public parks can be dated from the completion of the Bowling Green, for it was the first created solely for recreation.

By the middle of the eighteenth century, the public commons came to benefit people more than animals. Carl Bridenbaugh describes these areas as places where "a colonial could find some relief as well as pleasure, fresh air, and green grass." Boston Common was enclosed by a fence to prevent wild animals or mischievous people from misusing the ground. "The Parade at Newport at this time ceased to be a grazing area as more and more town houses . . . appeared in the neighborhood. The railed-in Bowling

Green proved a blessing to New Yorkers who passed the evening hours there or in the 'fine gardens and terrace walks' close by Fort George, from which there was a delightful view of the bay." Similarly, it was the Philadelphia commons where the townspeople diverted themselves.[4]

The growth of commerce and manufacturing in the period from 1790 to 1835 brought vast concentrations of people to the cities and caused concern among those opposed to urban growth. Despite these growing concentrations of people in larger cities the wealthy still had convenient access to the countryside and recreation. It was the poorest workingmen to whom recreational places were increasingly unavailable because they lacked the means of transportation to outlying open space.

In the older cities rapid and extensive building development left few opportunities for municipal governments to set aside land for public use. It also provided them with excellent excuses for continued inaction. Unfortunately, the pattern was similar in the new cities of the West, described by Richard C. Wade, where planning could have been more readily implemented. Wade notes that new cities like Pittsburgh, Cincinnati, and St. Louis usually sold off public grounds to raise funds to finance needed improvements. It was not until the 1820s that protests against this practice were heard. It was much later before the cities stopped the sales.[5]

By the early 1820s a parochial spirit of sectionalism with its fierce competitiveness was a major trend in the nation. With it came a more specific manifestation in the form of the booster spirit, a local pride. Daniel J. Boorstin has called this booster spirit a way of "thought and life which arose from how . . . communities grew, from how fast they grew, from their hopes and illusions, from their sense of destiny, from their reaching for the future."[6] More and more this competitiveness resulted in plans to improve the physical condition of the area. The appearance of the city was recognized as having a bearing on its ability to attract new residents.

A seemingly limitless destiny evoked intense effort from the city boosters. Their city was thought to outshine all others. This was the message the boosters told visitors, potential residents, and themselves. With such a mandate for material excellence, some citizens also called for a greater public concern for the necessities and amenities of civic and social life. Potential new residents and new businesses, which the boosters hoped to attract, were reluctant to establish roots unless living as well as business conditions were suitable. Yet, the cities, despite the eloquence of their champions, were slow to move. As the leading communities were changing from small towns to large urban centers and as this transformation reduced open space, pastoral settings, and the presence of nature that had always been available to urban dwellers everywhere, urbanites pondered the transformation to urbanism and sought means to lessen its impact. The discussion of parks figured in the contemporary debate over the relative virtues of town and country.

City boosters and others, who now began to see virtue in the city, saw in landscape design applied to the city a compensation for alleged evils of urban life. It was hoped that the blending of the city and country implicit in these designs would strengthen life patterns with the peace and security of rural qualities even though society was falling increasingly into an urban mold. New landscape ideals then becoming popular made common rural scenes the subject of artistic inquiry. What was studied and understood would be divided into its component parts. Some of these elements could be adapted to reruralize the appearance of the city. The ideal city would be an urban-rural continuum blending what tradition and morality deemed necessary for a proper style of life with what was clearly essential for growth, prosperity, and a rising standard of living. It became clear to those who chose to think about it that the two concepts were not mutually exclusive. The city could be a good place in which to live.[7]

Some people even went so far as to hold that an urban environment could be produced which would have superiority, not merely equality with the rural condition. In New York, Henry Whitney Bellows, pastor of the First Unitarian Church and, in the Civil War era, head of the United States Sanitary Commission, sought a city that if properly planned would be moral, healthy, and prosperous. The planning of cities took on new meanings. Bellows argued that the religious values basic to rural American could continue to influence populations provided the proper environment existed. Clearly, what was necessary was that proper environment. And it was thought that through the creation of parks this environment could be brought into reality.

The philosophical argument in support of the reruralization of the city attributed moral values to natural beauty, open space, fresh air, sunlight, and trees. Much of the acceptance of this assumption can be tied to the intellectual and artistic currents of the 1830s. The romantic school of painting, the republican movement in politics, and a growing attempt by organized religion to reconcile itself to the conditions of the city all helped create a climate of opinion that was receptive to the remaking of the city structure for social purposes. Basic to any such remolding would be the reruralization of the cityscape.[8]

Thomas Cole's landscape paintings gave visual representations to the intellectualized ideals of early "urban naturalists" like Dr. David Hosack and Andre Parmentier and of William Cullen Bryant, who by the early 1840s was editorializing in his *New York Post* for the development of city "retreats." The famous Hudson River school of Cole, Frederick E. Church, Henry Inman, and William S. Mount placed romantic landscapes before the public eye. These developments touched responsive chords among urban dwellers who had seen city growth diminish the influence of nature in their daily lives.[9]

Such divergent thinkers as John Ruskin, William Ellery Channing, Walt Whitman, Ralph Waldo Emerson, and Henry David Thoreau saw good coming from the return of nature to every American's environment.[10] The mind, spirit, and body of man, it was argued, could be improved in the city. Religious conservatism was undergoing a change as a result of the transcendental and unitarian doctrines that emerged to challenge it. Popular education through lyceums, libraries, and mechanics societies rose in importance as the nation went through the era of Jacksonian democracy, with its avowed concern for the common man. Finally, the earliest stage of an urban improvement effort could be detected, working to restructure the physical city along lines which would help in this elevation of the total man to new heights of morality, intellect, and health. By the early 1840s one could almost find a cohesive effort, an "urban trilogy" of mind, soul, and body. Although the trilogy was yet to define its specific principles, it was already evident that it carried a great amount of social responsibility. Man was going to look to nature, as John Ruskin had urged, to find materials and designs with which to build the modern city.

The romanticism of the 1830s was able to influence nature in the city in a way impossible in rural regions. J. B. Jackson, writing in *Landscapes*, asserts that ironically "the Romantic environment remained an urban and suburban phenomenon. Whereas the Jeffersonian concern for man as a social being determined the character of our whole rural landscape, the Romantic feeling for solitude and for closeness to unspoiled nature was confined to the middle-class urban citizen of the Eastern seaboard." In the city, nature could be used as an adjunct of man's environment. The urban situation was dynamic. It could be manipulated, and toward positive ends, it was hoped. On the contrary, rural America was so caught up in the agrarian myth that this idea actually became its mode of life.[11]

Thus the reruralization of the city was no longer just the embodiment of an aesthetic dream of a few men who wanted trees planted and open squares set apart. It was a manifestation of social engineering. But while the ideas were widely expressed, they were still far from being universally accepted. And even more important, even when accepted there was still no assurance that sympathetic programs would be carried out. The so-called park idea had become part of the larger effort to reform and remake the city. The manifestations of nature were so obviously absent in the city and were already considered so important to a civilized community that their appearance became the focal point of many of the reform efforts. It was in this climate of opinion, based on the messages of the Romantic school of art and the writing of those favorably disposed to a reruralized city, that park advocates worked.

Sir Isaac Newton proposed that a body at rest tends to stay at rest. In many ways this concept well applies to the municipal governments in the United States. In most instances, they were slow to accept responsibility for what already had become public necessities. Police, health, and fire protection, building and zoning regulation, school, library, and park development were almost always substandard in terms of community needs. Of course, much of this can be attributed to local control over the tax rate. Unlike federal or state budgets, which were seldom under the direct influence of those affected, American municipalities were constantly faced with opposition from conservative citizens, who recoiled at the thought of increased assessments. The result was a great reluctance on the part of city administrators to have the municipality undertake new functions. Despite this inaction, public needs had to be met. The formula most often used was for private enterprise to attempt to provide what was needed. The park movement was such a case. Early proposals for publicly financed parks almost always met with defeat. Into this vacuum stepped private promoters with alternative proposals for accomplishing the task.

By the mid-1830s, the city of Brooklyn, across the East River from New York, was also experiencing the consequences of urban growth.[12] For more than a decade Brooklyn's park advocates had sought governmental action to secure a promenade on the brow of the lofty, breezy heights—to no avail.

In Brooklyn the first tangible accomplishment of the park movement was hardly even noted as such when it occurred. Just as volunteer firemen put out fires while debate about municipal fire companies continued and a volunteer watch patrolled the city before an official police force was organized, the first provision for preserving a substantial parcel of natural landscape for the public use of urban dwellers came also from the private rather than the public sector. It was the creation of Green-Wood Cemetery from its inception in the mid-1830s onward that gave Brooklyn its first large refuge. And the use of that "quasi-park" was to influence deeply the course of the park movement in Brooklyn and elsewhere.

The first effort in the United States aimed at providing adequate urban burial plots in a pleasant environment was made by Doctor Jacob Bigelow of Boston in November of 1825. He proposed the establishment of a large, rural cemetery outside the city, with sufficient grounds to insure adequate room for generations to come. Despite general acceptance of this concept no definite progress was made until 1830 because of the lack of a suitable site. Curiously, it was interest in a totally different area that led to the establishment of the cemetery.

The Massachusetts Horticultural Society was founded in 1830. While considering various grounds for its gardens, the society developed an interesting scheme to ease its financial burdens. Well aware of the rural or "garden" concepts envisioned for a projected cemetery, the directors of the Horticultural Society proposed that part of the grounds selected for the gardens be used for interments.[13] Indeed, this appeared to be a perfect union of purpose, and it was readily agreed to by Bigelow, himself a leading botanist. Accordingly, in early 1831, Mount Auburn Cemetery was incorporated. On September 24, 1831, "in the presence of almost two thousand people," the cemetery–horticultural garden was consecrated. Public opinion favored the institution from its inception, and its success was assured. When the Horticultural Society, which originally owned the entire plot, expired, Mount Auburn had sufficient financial resources to buy the entire site.[14]

Thus America's first rural cemetery was established. In contrast to formal gardens then prevalent in the United States, the grounds at Mount Auburn were developed following the "picturesque" or "pastoral" ideal then in vogue in England. An early description of Mount Auburn notes that "the avenues are winding in their course and exceedingly beautiful in their gentle circuits, adapted picturesquely to the inequalities of the surface of the ground, and producing charming landscape effect." "Crowds" entered the grounds both to meditate and "to wander in a field of peace."[15] This sylvan beauty gained widespread fame both for its suitability as a cemetery and as a charming oasis free from commercial or city encroachment. Its lesson was well received throughout America, where problems as severe as those of Boston continued to exist.

Indeed, just as Bostonians had faced difficulty in selecting a proper site for their burial ground, New Yorkers and their neighbors in Brooklyn were at a loss to find a suitable location available at a reasonable price. While this difficulty delayed the inauguration of a cemetery project, the idea was hardly dormant. The lesson of Mount Auburn was well taken. Given the transformation of church lands to commercial purposes in the 1830s, burial sites in both New York City and Brooklyn became scarce. Even more discouraging was the disruption of graves as a result of urban encroachment. By the mid-1830s it was obvious that interment in neighborhood gravesites did not insure eternal slumber.[16] Nor was grave violation a preoccupation reserved for city planners or developers. Grave robbing was a common practice hardly hindered by the ineffective fences that surrounded the untended graveyards. Not only were churchyards proving inadequate to their consecrated purpose, but they were thought to foul the air and bring disease—principally yellow fever.

In the autumn of 1835, Major David B. Douglas joined with Henry E. Pierrepont, a prominent real estate owner and leading park advocate, to expedite a cemetery project. Together they reviewed various available sites and settled upon the hills of Gowanus, below Brooklyn.[17] It was the severe economic collapse of 1837 that finally enabled the garden cemetery project to achieve some tangible results as real estate prices plummeted, making the desired lands available at reasonable cost.

With the combined circumstances of depressed real estate prices and a continuing interest in the project, Douglas, Pierrepont, and other leading New Yorkers and Brooklynites in 1838 formed the Green-Wood Cemetery Corporation to purchase two hundred acres on Gowanus Hills. The act of incorporation, approved April 18, 1838, gave the cemetery the right to issue $300,000 in stock and to purchase a tract of land provided the City of Brooklyn gave its consent.[18] In a memorandum to the mayor and Common Council of Brooklyn, Douglas, Pierrepont, and Russell Stebbins appealed for approval of the desired site, arguing that it was a "location of extraordinary beauty and capability, and . . . superior to any other." The Council approved the request on the sixth of August. The *Long Island Star,* a consistent advocate of restoring nature to the city, expressed pleasure at the creation of Green-Wood, since until then Brooklyn had failed, in its opinion, to provide for the "undisturbed security of the dead." It viewed the projected cemetery as destined for success since it had been "wisely planned, on such liberal scale, as to ensure the objects in view." Only reluctance of the public to support the venture could prevent its completion.[19]

Financial considerations, especially in a period of depression, posed problems for Green-Wood's backers and at the outset threatened the enterprise. The difficulty of raising money through stock subscriptions beginning on November 3, 1838, led the commissioners, as the directors were called, to conclude that a joint-stock company was "not in harmony with an undertaking which, in its nature and aim, is eminently and essentially philanthropic." People apparently were reluctant to invest in what was a speculative venture. The cemetery corporation was therefore converted into an incorporated trust, exempted from taxes, but charged with applying all revenues either to payment for land purchases or maintenance of the grounds.[20]

Patronage of the enterprise was also hindered by the tradition of interment in long-held church yard plots; the unwillingness to be separated from persons buried earlier in these plots; and the distance of Green-Wood from New York and Brooklyn. Another restraint was cost. From the outset, single plots (large enough for a number of graves) sold for $100, while four or more were sold for $80 each. For those unable to purchase entire plots, the cemetery set aside what came to be known as the "public lots," where individual graves could be purchased for from $10 to $15 depending on the location.[21] Of course, since large plots would be bought in advance while single graves were purchased as needed, the corporation had to rely on the first source to accumulate capital. A number of churches purchased whole tracts and then sold graves as needed. In a few instances entire graveyards were removed to Green-Wood, permitting the sale of their city site.[22] In this way individuals could more readily afford interment in Green-Wood, and the arguments about separation of loved ones ended. Nevertheless, the subscription list remained unfilled, and without income the corporation was unable to meet its debts and secure complete title to the ground.[23] No interments could be permitted until all doubt about the ownership of the property was ended, and subscribers had no assurance that graves would be available in time of need. In the face of this uncertainty, proponents of the enterprise attempted to encourage support of it as a civic responsibility. In mid-1840, a correspondent of the *Star* urged public support, noting that "in order to ensure the success of an enterprise which in after years will redound to the praise and be the pride of their City, every individual must do something and that soon, to foster its existence."[24] Financial difficulties, by the summer of 1841 led the *Star* to assert that "Green-Wood cemetery . . . should claim the united zeal and interest of the two great cities which lie at its foot." It pointed to the disruption of the Baptist Churchyard on Gold Street in

New York for the extension of "contiguous streets" as another illustration of the way "bones and coffins are exposed or removed from their original positions . . . and subjected to the shuddering gaze of the sensitive, or the pitiless insult of the thoughtless and hardened." It cited Green-Wood as the only insurance people could have that their remains would not suffer the same fate.[25]

Anticipating a public meeting to raise funds, the *Brooklyn Daily News* asked why "the shady groves . . . lovely vallies [or] devious ways of this enchanting spot" did not induce more people to respond favorably to the subscription offerings. The editor documented the health hazards posed by city graveyards, so that the public might know in abandoning Green-Wood "we are sacrificing the health of the living."[26]

On the evening of March 14, 1842, approximately five hundred people crowded the Central Dutch Reformed Church on Henry Street in Brooklyn to hear an appeal for funds. The audience was told that a minimum of a hundred plots would have to be sold during the next week to keep the project viable. Speakers included clergymen, businessmen, and political leaders.[27] All emphasized first, the necessity of Green-Wood as a matter of health; second, the embellishment it would bring to the city; and third, the prestige it would attach to Brooklyn and New York. It is not known which of these arguments touched the audience, but that evening fifty-six subscriptions were sold.[28] In the days that followed, the *Daily News* and the *Brooklyn Eagle* both urged public support, and shortly the required subscriptions were sold and the future of the cemetery was assured. Less than two years later the vice-president of Green-Wood was able to note in his report that "the prospects of the Institution for the future are highly encouraging; its stability being no longer in doubt."[29]

Once the financial crisis had passed, subscriptions were taken in ever increasing number. Indeed, within three years Green-Wood was able to accumulate sufficient funds to enable it to propose the purchase of additional lands. Legislation enacted on May 11, 1846, provided for the addition of 125 acres to the 200 originally purchased.[30] By June of 1845, the thousandth plot had been sold. Many of the grave sites purchased in the early years were sought by relatives for those who were to be reinterred after removal from crowded churchyards. Indeed, of the 383 graves existing on December 31, 1843, more than 100 were reinterments from "downtown" cemeteries.[31] With the growth of the city, Green-Wood soon became the realm of an exclusive minority. As early as 1845, some 60 people owned nearly a third of the plots. That Green-Wood developed with a preponderance of large plots only reflects the general appeal of the grounds—and the ability of the wealthy to take advantage of it. Such was its appeal that plots were sold not only to residents of Brooklyn, New York City, upper New York State, nearby New Jersey and Connecticut, but as far afield as Philadelphia, New Orleans, Columbus, Ohio, and Washington, D.C.[32]

Green-Wood's site was "improved" as funds became available, but the scheme which was followed maintained a naturalistic setting. From the outset of the cemetery project, the directors, sitting as a design committee, decided that the grounds should resemble the peaceful countryside. Even the name "Green-Wood" was chosen because it spoke of "rural quiet, and beauty, and leafiness, and verdure." Indeed, an early suggestion to call the cemetery the Necropolis was rejected because "this word, however classical and ancient, conveys an ideal of *city* form and show" which the founders of the cemetery were particularly anxious to avoid.[33] In their choice of a name, the proprietors reflected the then current appeal of the mysterious and the natural which manifested itself in landscape design in the "picturesque" mode. Major Douglas, who actually designed the plan of the cemetery, took his cue from the example of Mount Auburn in Boston.

Until the 1830s American landscape design had been based on the European, classical model. Formalistic plantings of geometrically clipped plants constituted the popular style of the colonial and early national periods. Indeed, it was a great departure when people such as Brooklyn's Andre Parmentier began to assert the superiority of native plantings in natural settings. For unlike the rigid, specific forms then in use, the new style was a "composition of contours, colours, and forms." It took from the Chinese the respect for subtlety. In all, it was a pragmatic solution suitable to the American situation, where many of the plants familiar to European designers were not found and where large-scale earth moving and plantings were too costly. In the 1830s and 1840s the "new" American landscape designs began to emphasize the use of native materials in their natural conditions.[34] These designs were posited on the belief that Nature was the ultimate designer. The new designers responded to what Alexander Pope called for in his Epistle IV, written in 1731 at the start of the Romantic-rustic era. In describing how one should design a garden, he pleaded:

> In all, let Nature never be forgot,
> But treat the goddess like a modest fair,
> Nor overdress, nor leave her wholly bare;
> Let not each beauty everywhere be spied,
> Where half the skill is decently to hide.
> He gains all points, who pleasingly confounds,
> Surprises, varies, and conceals the bounds.[35]

The original ideal of the picturesque, "the mossy cells, old castles on cliffs and gloomy pines," was modified as time passed, especially after it crossed the Atlantic. As it emerged in the 1830s in America, "picturesque" meant naturalistic landscaping and in the realm of architecture, the gothic revival or neo-Palladian styles.

Not until the nineteenth century did Americans achieve fame for their garden designs. Before that, everything was copied from European patterns, and it was thus impossible to determine on which side of the Atlantic the plans had been drawn. The growing acceptance of naturalism was due in part to the efforts of patriotic naturalists, who wanted to develop a unique style of design that would be easily adapted throughout America. Parmentier was not the first to believe in such designs. He was, however, the first to advocate such ideas through extensive writings and lectures. Although he apparently had "very little understanding of the problems involved" and his actual gardens appear to have been overly romantic, his "influence was great and . . . inevitably established the basic type of planting in the New England area." Considering that Brooklynites had been greatly impressed with his horticultural garden, had listened to his lectures and had read his pamphlets, it is quite understandable that Major Douglas in his design for Green-Wood was sympathetic to a naturalistic design.[36]

From the point of view of its relationship to the park movement, the appeal of Green-Wood reflected the desire of urban dwellers for contact with nature. Certainly in its early years many visitors went to the grounds merely to enjoy the surroundings. The role of Green-Wood as a partial answer to Brooklyn's lack of parks had been brought before the public by the proponents of the cemetery in stressing its natural beauty. They noted in a letter to the *Star* how the grounds would be "laid out in good taste, and planted with shrubbery" so as to increase the "picturesque beauty of that part of the city."[37] That in addition to its utility as a cemetery Green-Wood would provide a landscaped open space was readily apparent.

What was unexpected was the extent to which visitors flocked to the grounds.

Although Green-Wood was within but a few miles of Brooklyn and New York, the journey to the hills of Gowanus, which included crossing Gowanus Creek by means of the Hamilton Avenue toll bridge, took at a minimum several hours. Thus it was not unusual for people to make the visit an all-day affair. They had little choice! Families and individuals responding to the invitation to view Green-Wood (as a prelude to purchasing plots—or so the trustees hoped) swarmed over the grounds. The *Star* urged such visits and described eight miles of carriage roads in the cemetery as offering "a delightful ride through shady groves, occasionally affording distant and extensive views." Green-Wood was not a morbid graveyard. Even before its financial status was secure, its grounds already were used for "excursions of pleasure and health." In 1839, Major Douglas noted that visitors "began to be attracted from the city in considerable numbers daily." When one remembers that as late as 1842 the corporation had to hold a public meeting to sell only a hundred plots, it is obvious that many of those who came to Green-Wood did not do so for business reasons.[38]

The beauties of the cemetery site drew great praise. Although city boosters called it one of the most beautiful places in the world, the more restrained noted that while Brooklyn had many beautiful locations capable of evoking pride, Green-Wood far exceeded all the rest in terms of "its extent, beauty and location." The *Star* thought it was destined to "become a popular and elegant place of resort, where some of the wild and lovely features of nature may be retained near the city." As early as 1841, Green-Wood drew the following comment from the *Daily News:*

We find no fault with those who like to bustle through life in a whirl of steam: but for our own part we love to dally on the road, to pluck a flower here, and plant one there, and while away a little of our time in the pursuit of pleasure, among sanctified creations of nature. There is a danger in being too utilitarian as well as an evil in being too speculative. But what is to prevent a combination of both? What merchant in New York—What professional man—What mechanic, but would feel better, physically and morally, to forget the season, the cares and toils incident to his pursuits, amidst the beauties of the Green-Wood Cemetery.

This suggestion of a resort on the Gowanus hills undoubtedly induced many people to travel to the grounds for recreational purposes. Certainly the number of visitors grew rapidly, and most apparently enjoyed what they found there.[39]

People went to Green-Wood to relax and spend a day out of doors. By doing so they also came to know the advantages a pastoral refuge could offer. An 1843 report describing the naturalistic design of the grounds noted that as an economy measure Green-Wood "was cultivated only in part, the forests being left to grow wilderness-like." In but a few years it became apparent that the lack of formal plantings was not at all objectionable. Speaking of the early 1840s, one commentator wrote that "in the variety and beauty of these grounds—so open and sunny in some parts—so shaded and secluded in others—so near to a vast city—yet so retired and still—Nature has left us nothing to desire."[40]

Because of insufficient funds no major planting or earth-moving schemes had been carried out. Yet, it was for their natural qualities that the grounds were recognized as giving urban dwellers access to an element increasingly absent from the city. Because of its natural beauty and subtle development, Green-Wood became America's best example of "picturesque" or "pastoral" landscape design, a status it was to retain until the development of Central Park in New York City.

Ultimately, as Green-Wood began to be increasingly used for its primary purpose, the public began to demand municipal action to insure the living would be able to enjoy as handsome a retreat as already existed for the dead. In the late 1850s and 1860s these demands were answered with the creation of New York's Central Park and, following the Civil War, Brooklyn's Prospect Park.

NOTES

1. Frederick Jackson Turner, *The Frontier in American History* (New York, 1958), p. 1.
2. Henry Nash Smith, *Virgin Land* (New York, 1950), p. 139, See also, Morton and Lucia White, *The Intellectual Versus the City* (New York, 1962), p. 14.
3. Carl Bridenbaugh, *Cities in the Wilderness* (New York, 1964), p. 21.
4. Carl Bridenbaugh, *Cities in Revolt* (New York, 1964), p. 36.
5. Richard C. Wade, *The Urban Frontier* (Chicago, 1964), pp. 28–29.
6. Daniel J. Boorstin, *The Americans: The National Experience* (New York, 1966), p. 114.

7. Peter J. Schmidt, *Back to Nature: The Arcadian Myth in Urban America* (New York, 1969), p. 67. See Roy Lubove's introduction to H. W. S. Cleveland, *Landscape Architecture as Applied to the Wants of the West* (Pittsburgh, 1965), p. vii. Peter P. Knights, "Population Turnover, Persistence and Residential Mobility in Boston, 1830–1860," Stephen Thernstrom and Richard Sennett, *Nineteenth Century Cities* (New Haven, 1969), pp. 258–60, 271–72, presents a statistical analysis of population mixture and growth in Boston. The work provides insight into many basic issues of the urban boom of the era 1830–60.

8. Schmidt, *Back to Nature,* p. 70; Hans Huth, *Nature and the American* (Los Angeles, 1957), pp. 42–44.

9. Huth, *Nature and the American,* pp. 46–48. See also Barbara Novak, *American Painting of the Nineteenth Century* (New York, 1969), pp. 61–71, 80–83, 86–87, and Richard McLanathan, *The American Tradition in the Arts* (New York, 1968), pp. 235–47.

10. *Ralph Waldo Emerson: A Profile,* ed. Carl Bode (New York, 1969), pp. xi–xii; Henry David Thoreau, "Paradise (To Be) Regained," *Thoreau, Principles, and Politics,* ed. Milton Meltzer (New York, 1963), p. 18.

11. J. B. Jackson, "Jefferson, Thoreau and After," *Landscapes,* ed. Ervin H. Zube, (Amherst, 1970), p. 6. Henry Nash Smith concludes that "the master symbol of the garden embraced a cluster of metaphors expressing fecundity, growth, increase, and blissful labor in the earth, all centering about the heroic figure of the idealized frontier farmer armed with that supreme agrarian weapon, the sacred plow." Leo Marx, in discussing this notion, says that "Americans, so far as they shared an idea of what they were doing as a people, actually saw themselves creating a society in the image of the garden." It was this rural image and resultant mode which carried on as the "agrarian myth" and nurtured anti-urban philosophies. Perhaps, as Marx contends, Jefferson "could not give full credence to that myth," but by the 1830s it had all the characteristics of a national spirit which if one measures its influence, was quite real. Smith, *Virgin Land,* p. 138; Leo Marx, *The Machine in the Garden* (New York, 1964), pp. 142–43.

12. Brooklyn's rate of growth was outstanding during the period 1800 to 1860. The decennial rates of increase for Brooklyn and New York are: 1800–10: 85.1 and 59.3; 1810–20: 63.0 and 28.4; 1820–30: 114.6 and 63.8; 1830–40: 135.4 and 54.3; 1840–50: 167.0 and 64.9; 1850–60: 88.5 and 57.8. Everett S. Lee and Michael Lali, "Population," *The Growth of Seaport Cities, 1790–1825* (Charlottesville, 1967), table 1, p. 27 and table 7, p. 41.

13. Cornelia W. Walter, *Mount Auburn Illustrated* (Boston, 1847), pp. 10–11. The grounds selected are in Cambridge on the banks of the Charles River and were purchased for $6,000 in 1831.

14. Foster W. Russell, *Mount Auburn Biographies* (Cambridge, 1953), p. xix; see also Walter, *Mount Auburn Illustrated,* p. 11; and Boorstin, *National Experience,* p. 19.

15. Walter, *Mount Auburn Illustrated,* p. 14. See Edward Mallins, *English Landscaping and Literature, 1660–1840* (London, 1966), pp. 36–44.

16. The public press reported numerous instances in which existing graves were disturbed. Many families discouraged by these practices purchased plots in Mount Auburn or Laurel Hill Cemetery in Philadelphia, which was modeled on Mount Auburn.

17. Henry R. Stiles, *The History of the City of Brooklyn,* 3 vols. (Brooklyn, 1867–70), 3:637; Nehemiah Cleaveland, *Green-Wood: A Directory for Visitors* (Brooklyn, 1851), p. 244; Nehemiah Cleaveland, *Green-Wood Cemetery, A History of the Institution* (New York, 1866), pp. 6–8, 168.

18. "An Act to incorporate the Greenwood Cemetery," *Laws of the State of New York,* Sixty-first session, chapter 298, pp. 297–99. The act appointed as

"Commissioners of Greenwood" Samuel Ward, John P. Stagg, Charles King, David B. Douglas, Russell Stebbins, Joseph A. Perry, Henry E. Pierrepont, and Pliny Freeman.

19. Cleaveland, *Green-Wood Cemetery*, p. 171. The site was between Eighteenth and Thirty-fourth streets, from the Brooklyn-Flatbush line to a line running midway between Fifth and Sixth avenues. *Long Island Star*, June 25, 1838.

20. Cleaveland, *Green-Wood Cemetery*, pp. 179-80; *Star*, March 14, 1829; "An Act to Alter and Amend 'An Act to incorporate the Greenwood Cemetery'," *Laws of the State of New York*, Sixty-second Session, chapter 156, pp. 131-33.

21. *Green-Wood Cemetery: Its Rules, Regulations, etc. With an Appendix Containing a Catalogue of the Proprietors, etc.* (New York, 1845), pp. 10-11, 24-25.

22. Cleaveland, *Green-Wood Cemetery*, pp. 26, 29-30. Among the institutions purchasing large plots for the convenience of their memberships were the Odd Fellows, American Seamen's Friend Society, Christ Church, First Presbyterian Church of Brooklyn, and the First Unitarian Congregational Church of Brooklyn.

23. *Star*, September 16, 1829; Cleaveland, *Green-Wood Cemetery*, pp. 23-24; David B. Douglas, *Exposition of the Plan and Objects of the Green-Wood Cemetery* (New York, 1839), p. 15.

24. *Star*, June 15, 1840. Green-Wood was not able to meet daily operating costs, let alone its outstanding debt. For the year ending July 1, 1840, (the first year for which books were kept), there were expenses of $7,800.86 and receipts of $3,791.00. For the seventeen months ending December 1, 1841, expenses totaled $3,112.05 and there were no receipts. During the next twelve months, $20,704.39 was spent and $18,455.72 was received. In the next three years minor losses were still recorded, after which, with few exceptions, receipts exceeded expenses by a wide margin. Cleaveland, *Green-Wood Cemetery*, pp. 207, 211.

25. *Star*, August 5, 1841.

26. *Brooklyn Daily News*, March 14, 1842.

27. *Daily News*, March 14, 1842; *Star*, August 5, 1841.

28. Among the speakers, in addition to the directors of Green-Wood, were the Reverend Doctor Samuel H. Cox of the First Presbyterian Church, the Reverend Frederick A. Farley of the Unitarian Church, George Hall, ex-mayor of Brooklyn, Abiel A. Low, Brooklyn merchant, Arthur Tappan, New York merchant and later staunch abolitionist, and Richard Upjohn, New York architect. Cleaveland, *Green-Wood Cemetery*, pp. 182-83; *Daily News*, March 15, 1842; Stiles, *Brooklyn*, 3:79.

29. *Daily News*, March 15, 1842; *Brooklyn Eagle*, March 15, 1842; *Daily News*, June 17, 1842. Joseph A. Perry, *Green-Wood Cemetery, Report of the Vice-President, December 4, 1843* (New York, 1844), p. 11.

30. "An Act to Amend an act entitled 'An Act to Incorporate the Green-Wood Cemetery' passed April 18, 1838," *Laws of the State of New York*, Sixty-ninth Session, chapter 329, p. 469. Cleaveland, *Green-Wood Cemetery*, p. 184.

31. *Green-Wood Cemetery Register of Interments Number One*, September 5, 1840-April 30, 1850, Numbers 1 to 9988, filed in the record room of the Green-Wood Cemetery, Fifth Avenue and Twenty-fifth Street, Brooklyn, pp. 1-6 and 6-15, passim. The cemeteries from which bodies were removed include New York Marble Cemetery, Wall Street Presbyterian Church, Reformed Dutch Church on Houston Street, Brick Church, Second Avenue Presbyterian Church, Rutgers Street Burial Ground, and St. Mark's Church.

32. *Green-Wood Cemetery, Its Rules, Regulations, etc.*, pp. 43-50, passim.

33. Cleaveland, *Green-Wood Cemetery*, p. 14.

34. Christopher Hussey, *English Gardens and Landscapes, 1700-1750* (New York,

1967), p. 39; Christopher Hussey, *The Picturesque: Studies in a Point of View* (London, 1927), pp. 155–56. See also Charles E. Brownell, "In the American Style of Italian: The E. C. Litchfield Villa" (unpublished M.A. thesis, the Winterthur Museum, 1969), pp. 17–18, 22.

35. Alexander Pope, "Epistle IV, To Richard Boyle, Earl of Burlington," lines 50–56. See also Mallins, *English Landscaping and Literature,* chapter 2, "Kent, Burlington, Pope and Friends," pp. 26–48.

36. Mallins, *English Landscaping and Literature,* pp. 142–43; Derek Clifford, *A History of Garden Design* (New York, 1963), p. 302; Cleaveland, *Green-Wood Cemetery,* p. 26.

37. Letter of David B. Douglas, Russell Stebbins, Henry E. Pierrepont, and Pliny Freeman, *Star,* August 13, 1838.

38. *Star,* July 15, 1839. In modern times the beauties of the grounds are still advertised. A recent notice stated that "noted for the beauty of its plantings . . . here, within the city limits, is a rare display of flowering trees, shrubs, and bushes. Bring the family and stroll along the winding tree-shaded paths and roadways to enjoy the serenity and beauty of the grounds. You will find it a pleasant experience." *New York Times,* May 16, 1968, 47:7.

39. *Daily News,* May 3, 1841; *Star,* July 31, 1841; *Daily News,* March 15, 1842. This comment was published as part of a lengthy essay aimed at persuading people to purchase lots in the cemetery during the period of crisis.

40. Perry, *Green-Wood Cemetery, Report of the Vice-President,* p. 9; Cleaveland, *Green-Wood Cemetery,* p. 146.

EIGHT HOURS AND THE BRICKLAYERS' STRIKE OF 1868 IN NEW YORK CITY

For the labor movement of the 1860s, the eight-hour day was a key objective. Trade unions regarded shorter hours as basic to their success, and since many employers shared labor's views of the results to be expected, the shorter day was most difficult to win. Although Ira Steward is the best-known exponent of the importance of the eight-hour day, his theory of shorter hours had critical elements that were not adopted by the trade unions. Steward's stress on the beneficent role of mechanization, his emphasis upon political action as the primary means for securing eight hours, and his effort to tie shorter hours to a millennial objective found little support among the leaders of the trade unions. For them, the movement for eight hours had several well-understood and clearly defined purposes, even without the influential contribution of Steward as a theorist and publicist.[1] It is our purpose to examine the reason why trade unions desired eight hours so strongly, and to discuss one of the major efforts to secure it—the bricklayers' strike of 1868 in New York City.

The attraction of eight hours to trade unions rested upon two expected results: an improvement in the quality of life for the worker, and the positive effects upon the supply of labor.

The results of shorter hours upon workers had been widely debated since the ten-hour movement of the 1830s. Opponents contended that shorter hours would lead to a decline in the total amount of goods available and an increase in price. This would ultimately reduce the American standard of living. In addition, idleness would increase vice and drunkenness. Opponents appealed to the traditional American values of hard work and long hours, which were so intimately connected to the rural origin of the nation. The economic progress of the country, the morality of its people, and traditional values all were threatened by fewer hours of labor.

Supporters of shorter hours met this defense of the existing workday squarely. They contended that it was long hours, not less work, that imperiled the nation. Edward Rogers, the labor representative on the commission in Massachusetts that investigated the hours of labor in 1867, argued that eight hours would lead not to drunkenness and vice, but to a greater interest in religion and literature.[2] In the same year, C. W. Gibson, the corresponding secretary of the National Labor Union, stressed the importance of shorter hours in allowing workers the "mental culture, social advantages and refreshing rest" that they deserved.[3] Less time spent at work also made it more feasible for workers to live some distance from their employment. This opened the possibility of leaving the crowded older tenement districts of major cities for the new residential areas.[4] For labor leaders, eight hours meant enlightenment, not idleness; uplift, not vice; and social improvement, not personal degradation. This line of argument was probably the most popular one used by the defenders of shorter hours, and it often attracted support outside the labor movement.

Whatever the personal advantages for workers, eight hours also had an effect upon the existing class structure in the nation. Drawing upon a major demand of trade unions in the 1830s, labor spokesmen in the 1860s argued that long hours prevented workers from achieving the equality due American citizens. Excessive hours of toil, argued J. C. Whaley, president of the National Labor Union, dragged down American workers "from the high position of republican freemen to the degraded one of voiceless slaves." Eight hours would allow workers to educate themselves, and thereby to overcome the inferiority attached to ignorance. It would also allow workers to participate more fully in the political process, which would lead to an increase in the number of workers serving in law-making bodies.[5]

However important these arguments for the eight-hour day, it was clear by the 1860s that the role of eight hours in alleviating the excess of labor in the market had become the most important consideration for trade union leaders. Shorter hours would mean a reduction in unemployment, both seasonal and long-term. Since trade union leaders believed wages and other conditions of employment were set by supply and demand, eight hours would enhance the bargaining power of labor by requiring the employment of more workers to maintain the existing level of production.

This would ultimately allow wages to rise, and it would become easier to conduct strikes and organize workers. Drawing upon Steward's arguments, trade union leaders also pointed out that eight hours would increase total consumption as employment rose. This increase in total purchasing power would encourage output and reduce the likelihood of overproduction and economic depression. Thus, labor leaders maintained that eight hours would not mean fewer goods and a lower standard of living, but greater production and a better life for all based upon full employment.

These benefits of the eight-hour day were clearly stated during the early 1860s by labor spokesmen. Jonathan Fincher, the leading labor editor of the early 1860s, wrote that the problem of excess labor had been discussed at union conventions even before the Civil War.[6] The war made the situation worse in the long run, for though workers found employment during wartime, Fincher foresaw an excess of labor once the soldiers returned to the work force.[7] In New York City, his prediction was borne out by a surplus of labor from the end of the war through 1867.[8] Eight hours was a major weapon against this development. William Sylvis, president of the Iron Molders' International Union, and later president of the National Labor Union, pointed out in 1864 that diminishing the hours of labor "is to multiply the number of laborers."[9] As a letter-writer argued in *Fincher's Trades' Review* in 1864, eight hours would

increase the demand for labor, for no *honest* man can do as much work in eight hours as he has been doing in ten; consequently, it will require a force two-tenths stronger than before—that is, where eight men were employed, two additional ones will have to be added. This being the case, and no one can deny its truth, we will have little difficulty in *raising wages* above the present standard.[10]

The agitation for the eight-hour day began in earnest after the end of the Civil War, and it continued, more or less forcefully, until the depression of the 1870s destroyed much of the labor movement. These were years in which trade union leaders believed that the supply of labor was on the increase as immigration rose, employers constantly sought to add more apprentices, and more Americans moved from rural areas to cities. At the same time, the protection that skill had offered against such competition weakened as division of labor made the artisan less important. In this period, labor spokesmen continued to stress that a reduction of hours would mean increased employment.[11] The president of the Coopers'

International Union argued in 1870 that the excess of workers in the trade, in part a result of mechanization, could be offset by a reduction to eight hours. Such a change would employ one-fifth more workers than the ten-hour day.[12] In the following year, the Workingmen's Union of New York City called for eight hours. The resolution made it clear that "the diminution of the hours of labor will make a greater demand for labor, thereby supplying all with the necessaries of life."[13] During 1872, a massive wave of strikes in New York City occurred over the demand for eight hours, and once again the effect of shorter hours on the labor supply was widely discussed. In this case, machinery was also cited as a cause of distress among workers.[14] Clearly, trade unions understood the economic benefits that they wanted from eight hours, but to translate this into effective action was quite another matter.

The major obstacles to the eight-hour movement were the resolute opposition from employers and the coolness of many workers, who feared wage reductions and believed that long and bitter strikes would be required to secure the shorter day.

Trade unionists envisioned an increase in employment proportionate to the decrease in the number of hours. This meant that productivity had to remain the same. If productivity increased, the need for a greater work force would be reduced, or even eliminated. Thus trade union leaders assumed no significant immediate increase in productivity in their statements during the 1860s about the value of eight hours to the worker. Yet this basic assumption roused the strongest opposition from employers, as well as a denial from some supporters of eight hours.

Employers often accepted the contention of the trade union leaders that shorter hours would mean no immediate increase in productivity. Accordingly, the cost of production would rise, and ultimately this would mean higher prices for the consumer, or lower profits for employers should competition prevent the translation of the higher cost into higher prices. Of course, wages could be reduced in proportion to the reduction of hours. However, most employers rejected this course, even when workers were prepared to accept a wage reduction along with a reduction of hours. In this regard, they again accepted the argument of the supporters of eight hours that any decrease in wages would be only temporary. If shorter hours did soak up excess labor, the law of supply and demand would soon lead to an increase in wages.[15] The employers in New York City rejected the offer of the bricklayers in 1868 to reduce wages approximately 10 percent as hours were cut from ten to eight.

One of the leaders of the employers' association argued that once hours had been reduced, the bricklayers would demand the wages then paid for ten hours. He also did not expect any immediate increase in productivity. On the contrary, he claimed that productivity had dropped during the 1860s from two thousand bricks per day to one thousand. Another employer charged that seven hundred bricks per day was a better average figure.[16] Under these circumstances, many employers chose to fight the demand for eight hours.

Some supporters of eight hours argued that workers would immediately increase their productivity. Ira Steward believed that the opposition of employers would be reduced if they were convinced that workers would do as much in eight hours as in ten.[17] Yet even Steward recognized that such an increase was usually dependent upon the introduction of machinery. However, most trades in the 1860s were not mechanized, and Steward realized that in those that already used sophisticated machinery, the productivity of workers was tied to the speed of the equipment, which normally was set at the most profitable level. In this situation, a decrease in hours would mean a decrease in production.[18]

Ultimately, the productivity issue moved beyond economic considerations and became a matter of basic political values. If pushed to the limit on productivity, Fincher posed the key question when he asked:

Shall the wealth of the country, as told in dollars and cents, be increased at the cost of the worth, virtue and manhood among the majority of our citizens, or shall our national growth in wealth be less rapid?[19]

In answer, trade union leaders offered a sufficiency of output in place of maximum production. They believed that in eight hours workers would still produce more than enough to meet the needs of all—without an immediate increase in productivity. Moreover, the shorter workday would provide basic benefits to workers and ultimately be of advantage to the entire society.

The opposition of employers was also the result of the relative permanence of changes in hours. Reductions in the workday during the first half of the nineteenth century had become an accepted standard. Unlike wages, which fluctuated in response to economic conditions and the market for labor, as well as the relative strength of the employers and workers, hours tended to remain fixed. This reduced the flexibility that employers had in controlling their cost of production. In the late nineteenth century, employers would often provide wage increases, when pressed by their workers, but at the same time they would refuse to reduce hours or to recognize unions—both of which would have meant fundamental changes in the way a company could operate in the future.

The hostility of employers to eight hours led to the fear among workers that it would be conceded, if at all, only with a proportionate cut in wages. Most workers could ill afford such a reduction.[20] As we have noted, the bricklayers did propose a pay reduction of approximately 10 percent along with their demand for eight hours, and the Carpenters' and Joiners' National Union recommended eight hours to its locals in 1868 at "a proportionate reduction in wages." All labor spokesmen argued that any such reduction was purely tactical. It would help reduce the opposition among employers, but once eight hours was achieved, the law of supply and demand would lead wages to increase again. The Carpenters' and Joiners' Union envisaged that the rise would be proportionate to the cut in hours— i.e., 20 percent.[21] Yet many workers were unprepared to accept the theory that called for a wage reduction in the present in anticipation of wage increases in the future. Moreover, strikes for shorter hours were often bitter and prolonged. It was easier to settle for the wage increase frequently offered by employers in lieu of a reduction in hours. Accordingly, very few strikes in the 1860s were on the issue of hours. In New York City, from 1861 to 1873, only 70 of 249 strikes that were tradewide occurred because of a dispute over hours. If the wave of strikes in 1872 is excepted, only 17 of 151 strikes were over hours. Wages were far and away the major issue in strikes.[22] Thus a major effort to secure eight hours, such as the bricklayers' strike of 1868, had great importance as a test of the ability of trade unions to win this crucial demand.

The campaign for eight hours proceeded on two fronts: trade unions sought to establish a shorter day through their own efforts, and the labor movement, including these same unions, demanded legislation to set eight hours as the standard workday. These two approaches were not mutually exclusive, although some leading supporters of eight hours, such as Ira Steward and Andrew Cameron, the editor of the *Workingman's Advocate,* an influential labor newspaper, strongly favored political action. Cameron viewed strikes as generally ineffective, and he sought to have eight hours serve as a major impetus to independent political action by the labor movement.[23] However, trade union leaders initially turned to action by their own organizations. As the committee that reported to the convention of the Plasterers' National Union in 1866 put it, although many regarded the eight-hour question as one to be adjusted by law, they believed it to be a matter for "each branch or society of labor, and that it should not be dragged in the mire of party politics."[24]

In New York City, trade union leaders followed a similar course. In the discussion of eight hours that took place in the city's labor movement during 1864 and 1865, the stress was on trade union action, not legislation. On February 2, 1866, the Workingmen's Union—the central labor body for New York City—called upon local trade unions to strike for eight hours as of March 10, 1866. The state central labor body—the Workingmen's Assembly—also supported immediate steps for eight hours. However, the only unions to take up this call were those representing shipyard workers and house painters.[25]

The strike by the skilled workers in the shipyards during the spring of 1866 was recognized as the "first clearly defined attempt of workingmen to enforce the eight hour system of labor."[26] The workers did not offer to reduce their wages in exchange for eight hours. Employers rejected the demand, and ultimately four thousand workers in New York City joined the strike. Trade unions in New York City and the eastern United States contributed to the strike fund; support and encouragement came from throughout the labor movement; and fellow shipyard workers in Boston, Portsmouth (New Hampshire), and Philadelphia struck when ships from New York City were brought to their yards for repairs. Yet the strike was lost after seven weeks.[27] Clearly a strike for eight hours required unprecedented resources, and one disgruntled ship carpenter complained that despite the outside aid, more should have been made available "from our fellow workingmen throughout the country whose battle we were fighting as well as our own."[28]

The failure of the strike by the shipyard workers led the trade unions in New York City to turn to political action in 1867. The New York state legislature passed legislation on hours that was typical of the period. It set eight hours as the legal day's work, but allowed workers to contract for longer hours.[29] Although weak, the law did give sanction to the demand for eight hours. However, trade unions had to make the essentially hortatory law into an actual condition of employment.[30] The strike was the vehicle for achieving this. The Workingmen's Union of New York City warned that workers would invoke the eight-hour law by November 1867, but only the well-organized plasterers struck for the shorter day. After a short stoppage in August 1867, employers conceded eight hours for the moment.[31]

The bricklayers made the next major effort for eight hours in the summer of 1868. The failure of this strike, and unfavorable trade conditions, led the labor movement in New York City to shift back to political action during the years 1869 to 1871. Further legislation on eight hours was less an objective than protection against conspiracy suits and stronger laws on apprentices.[32] In 1872, trade unions in New York City resumed the active campaign for eight hours, and a massive wave of strikes took place.[33] Although many unions initially won eight hours as a result of these strikes, the gains were soon lost. Thus political action and trade union action were not exclusive approaches, but tactical steps, to be used in whatever combination best met the needs of the moment.

A number of national unions debated eight hours at their conventions. The expected endorsement of the shorter day was joined with considerable hesitancy over concrete steps to achieve it. The National Typographical Union divided closely on the issue of recommending eight hours to its locals as of a stated date—May 1, 1866.[34] The plasterers called for the eight-hour day at their convention in 1865, but in cooperation with other trades.[35] Despite the success of the plasterers' local in New York City, which gained the shorter day in 1867, by 1868 only three locals of the eighteen that reported to the national convention of the union had won eight hours.[36] The carpenters were warned in 1865 and 1867 to be wary of strikes for the eight-hour day that would leave the union "more or less demoralized."[37] As we shall see, the Bricklayers' National Union gave very little support to the locals in New York City that were striking for eight hours in 1868. The strong opposition of employers to shorter hours, the lack of sizable strike funds in locals, the controversy between national officers and locals over the creation of national strike funds, and the fear of national and local leaders that their unions could be destroyed by involvement in a continuing series of strikes over eight hours, explain why trade unions were cautious about pressing their demands for the shorter day. Thus each effort to win eight hours was important. Most significant of all the actions in the 1860s was the strike by the bricklayers in New York City. The stoppage began in June 1868 and lasted through the entire summer construction season. It became the major test case for the viability of the demand for eight hours.

Tradewide strikes were a common occurrence in New York City during the 1860s, and the success rate was high. However, most of these strikes concerned wages. As we have noted, the few strikes over hours before 1868 produced mixed results. The bricklayers' effort promised success.

There had been continuous local organization among bricklayers in New York City through the 1860s, and a national union existed as well. Estimates placed approximately 75 percent of the bricklayers of New York City in three locals. They were sound financially and could command a substantial strike fund. In fact, membership was sufficient to allow for an initiation fee of as much as $25 in the year before the strike. This was a high sum for the period, and, by contrast, it dropped to $5 in 1869 after the strike reduced membership and depleted the treasuries of the locals. Economic conditions were also good in the construction industry. Increased immigration following the end of the Civil War stimulated residential building, and many firms decided to replace old structures in lower Manhattan with new buildings. Furthermore, the labor movement of New York City was vigorous throughout the 1860s. A significant number of trade unions survived for a period of from seven to a dozen years. In terms of both number of local trade unions, and continuity, the labor movement in New York City was the major one in the nation.[38] Active central labor bodies in both the city and state added one more bit of strength. Thus the bricklayers of New York City seemed to be an ideal group of workers to lead the way to eight hours.

The strike for eight hours was not entered into lightly. The reluctance displayed by other unions also was found among the bricklayers. The national convention of the bricklayers' union in January 1868 made it clear that strikes were a necessary, though hazardous, undertaking, and there was discussion of establishing a national strike fund.[39] However, strikes for eight hours were considered separately. Locals from New York City, Brooklyn, and Albany called on the national union to support such strikes. Delegates were well aware that a strike for eight hours by the St. Louis local in 1867 had failed. Moreover, strikes of all sorts were so common in 1867 that the president's frequent calls for assessments had produced hostility in many locals. In fact, the convention eliminated the president's power to levy assessments, and instead required a two-thirds vote of the locals in a referendum.[40]

The committee that considered the eight-hour issue submitted minority and majority reports. The minority report argued that the national union should support locals in strikes for the eight-hour day. It was defeated by a vote of 40 to 46. The majority report voiced approval of the eight-hour day in principle, but considered it "inexpedient at the present time" to aid locals that struck for eight hours since this would weaken the national union. The convention divided on this report, but it was ultimately defeated by a vote of 42 to 43. The desire for eight hours and the difficulty of securing it clashed in the minds of the delegates. Finally a resolution was unanimously adopted that merely recognized local strikes for eight hours and pledged "all the assistance that lies in our power."[41] Placing the issue of support for local strikes on a voluntary basis eliminated the controversy. As we shall see, such voluntary aid was to be a significant factor in the strike of 1868, but clearly the bricklayers were wary of committing themselves to a full-fledged effort for eight hours.

This wariness also was reflected in the call for the strike in New York City in June of 1868. The smallest of the three locals, No. 12, composed of German-speaking bricklayers, debated the eight-hour issue and finally decided to maintain the ten-hour day, if wages of $5 per day were paid.[42] Once the strike was under way, Local No. 12 split. Half of the membership left, formed the German Ten Hour Bricklayers' Association, and agreed to work ten hours if the wages were set at $5.00 to $5.50 per day.[43]

Not only the German bricklayers had doubts about the strike. The three locals in New York City met jointly to vote on the strike. A motion to table the strike call was lost by a scant majority of three, and the strike call itself carried by only a two-thirds vote.[44]

The opposition from within the rank and file can be explained on two grounds. First, bricklayers feared a long strike because of the importance of the eight-hour issue and the probable opposition of the employers. The resistance of the employers became apparent almost immediately after the strike began. The employers formed an association to combat the strike. Although not all the employers joined, enough did to make it clear that eight hours could not be won without the concurrence of the association. J. T. Connover, who was elected president, made it clear that he not only opposed the eight-hour demand, but that the strike was a turning point "in the great labor movement that has agitated the country for several years."[45] Some employers objected to the existing limits on apprentices, or simply to dictation by trade unions.[46] Thus the most antilabor elements among the employers viewed eight hours as the issue on which to make a determined effort to weaken the union.

Second, many workers were cool to the strike because of the decision to offer a reduction in daily wages (from $5.00 to $4.50) in exchange for eight hours. The wage reduction was an inducement to employers to forego a strike, and labor leaders argued ceaselessly that any wage concession in conjunction with the shorter day would soon be made up. Eight hours also provided the springboard for further wage gains. However, many workers were skeptical. Thus the bricklayers entered the strike with misgivings, but once the struggle was on, they fought for eight hours throughout an entire summer construction season. And once the strike was on, the leaders of the labor movement rushed to support the bricklayers.

Labor spokesmen made clear how important they judged the bricklayers' strike to be. Andrew Cameron wrote an editorial in support of the stoppage despite his objection to strikes as the focus of action by workers. The bricklayers' strike had become the test case for eight hours: success in New York City would lead to success elsewhere; failure would set back the entire movement for the shorter day—perhaps for years. Accordingly, Cameron urged the vice-presidents of the National Labor Union to appeal for financial support for the bricklayers. William Jessup, president of the Workingmen's Assembly of New York State, also feared failure for the bricklayers would mean that "the Eight Hour system is defeated for years." Those locals of plasterers and painters which already had won eight hours would probably lose their gains as well. Beyond this, Jessup believed that the strike had become a test of the ability of trade unions to win a significant demand through strike action, and defeat would weaken the trade union movement as a whole.[47]

A massive rally in support of the bricklayers was called by the Workingmen's Assembly on August 12, 1868. It was preceded by a procession of two thousand persons. At the rally, Alexander Troup, of the Typographical Union, stressed that the bricklayers were the advance guard of the workers in their demand for eight hours. Troup pointed out, as did the resolution passed at the meeting, that the bricklayers were simply enforcing the eight-hour law of New York. If they were to fail, such laws would be useless.[48]

The bricklayers also received support from the National Labor Union. Its council met on July 2, passed a resolution in support of the strikers "who are now suffering the consequences of their desire to respect the eight hour law of this state," and called for financial assistance from the labor movement. At the annual meeting of the National Labor Union in September 1868, the organization refashioned its policy on strikes to assist the bricklayers. In 1866, the National Labor Union had approved a position on strikes that stressed their use only as a tactic of last resort. The convention of 1868 modified this in favor of a milder statement. As the well-known labor leader Richard Trevellick pointed out at the convention, he was not abandoning his doubts about the effectiveness of the strike as a tool of the labor movement; yet he was willing to modify the existing provision in the platform "for the sake of his fellow-workmen of New York." Andrew Cameron also made clear that his basically negative attitude toward strikes was unchanged, and he believed that the existing policy would have been reaffirmed except for the strike of the bricklayers in New York. Under the circumstances, reaffirmation would have been hailed by the enemies of labor as an admission of the failure of the strike.[49]

Moral support of this sort was important for the bricklayers, but more crucial was concrete aid from the labor movement. This could be in the form of money or jobs. A number of bricklayers' locals offered to provide jobs for strikers. The Philadelphia local had places for 100 to 150 men. Bricklayers' unions in Brooklyn and Jersey City, among others, made similar offers.[50] After three weeks of the strike, the unions reported that 150 strikers had been sent to work in Philadelphia, from 50 to 60 had gone to Baltimore, and "a large number" had found employment in Boston. Others were working in localities around New York City.[51] Ultimately, the unions claimed a total of 1,000 men had left the city.[52] Since the membership of the three locals was estimated at 3,000, the movement of bricklayers to other areas significantly eased the burden on the strike fund. As the strike continued into September, and resources began to run thin, demands arose in the unions to stop strike benefits and ask idle workers to find employment out of town.[53] The offers of jobs by unions outside New York City was thus an important aid to the striking bricklayers.

Despite the exodus of strikers, there were still idle union members left in the city. These men received strike benefits from the very start of the strike. Although the benefits were later reduced, they continued throughout the summer.[54] This was most unusual for strikes in this period, and it was made possible not only by the funds that the locals had available prior to the strike, but because of financial assistance from the labor movement.

Financial appeals were a common feature of strikes in the 1860s. A significant amount had been contributed to the shipyard workers in their strike for eight hours in 1866. The tailors had spent $8,000 in a strike in New York City in 1864, which was raised by loans and donations from outside the union. Collections of $2,320 during a strike in New York City in 1863–64 had roused the attention of *Fincher's Trades' Review*.[55] The bricklayers reported contributions of $20,775 at the end of July, and the final financial report in November 1868 included "subscriptions" of

$29,801.75 and disbursements of $27,742.75.[56] At the height of the strike, the painters' local of Brooklyn and the stairbuilders' union promised their entire treasuries to the bricklayers. There were appeals by William Jessup to unions throughout New York State, and traveling committees were sent through the eastern half of the nation. One observer cited this unusual support as the clearest testimony to the popularity of the eight-hour system.[57]

Without doubt, the actual financial support received by the bricklayers was unprecedented for the period, and, without doubt, the strike was regarded by the labor movement as a key test of the viability of the eight-hour demand; but one must also recognize that financial aid was difficult for most unions in the 1860s, and, under close examination, the figures reveal a narrower base of financial support for the bricklayers than the overall totals suggest.

First, a significant proportion of the financial aid came from other locals of the bricklayers' union. Reported pledges and contributions from bricklayers in Brooklyn, Poughkeepsie, Yonkers, Kingston, Hoboken, Jersey City, Newark, New Haven, Boston, Washington, Baltimore, Pittsburgh, Indianapolis, and Dayton reached just under $8,000. These locals undoubtedly regarded success in the strike in New York City as essential for their own hopes for the eight-hour day.

In contrast to the support from locals of the bricklayers' union, the national union took no concrete steps to support the strike in New York City. As noted earlier, prior to the stoppage in New York, the issue of support for local strikes over eight hours had divided the delegates to the convention of the Bricklayers' National Union. Accordingly, president John Frost decided not to take the steps necessary for an assessment on behalf of the strikers in New York City.[58] There were even charges he had argued in the press that the strike was illegal. Frost denied this, and he received a vote of support from the largest of the three striking locals.[59] Clearly Frost was not prepared to draw the national union into support of the strike, and thus it was all the more significant that locals chose to contribute voluntarily.

The division within the Bricklayers' National Union over strikes for eight hours continued at the convention in January 1869. A resolution was offered to indemnify those bricklayers who had struck in New York City during 1868 at a rate of $7 a week. This payment acknowledged that the national union had erred in not supporting the strike. Passage of such a resolution would also herald support for future strikes. In the debate, those who wanted aid to strikes for eight hours argued it was the only way the shorter day could be won. Opponents charged that compulsory support of such strikes would divide the membership and weaken the national union. One delegate made it clear that should such a rule be adopted, "the members of this Union would not give a dime." Opponents wanted the existing system of voluntary contributions to continue. The division reflected the difference in interest between stronger locals, which believed they could win eight hours, especially with the support of the national union, and weaker locals, which were unprepared to force the issue of the shorter day in their own areas, and which feared a series of taxes to support efforts elsewhere. Ultimately, the resolution was defeated and the existing system retained.[60]

Proximity to the scene of the strike was a second major criterion of support. Beyond the ranks of the bricklayers, the most significant aid came from the plasterers' union of New York City, which had secured eight hours in 1867. Failure of the bricklayers' effort would endanger their gain, and, in fact, the plasterers had to return to ten hours in 1870. The plasterers contributed almost $5,000—a huge amount by any standard for the period.[61] Other unions in New York City and the surrounding area also regarded their chances for eight hours as linked to the bricklayers' strike. Financial support diminished significantly as the distance from New York City increased.

Third, the actual amount of money received by the striking unions, as compared to the amount pledged, could vary substantially. The strike committee's public announcements of aid were obviously designed to bolster morale among the workers as well as convince the employers that the bricklayers could stay out indefinitely. Thus the reports in the press of financial help from the Bricklayers' National Union were erroneous.[62] Of the $5,000 pledged by the Brooklyn local of bricklayers, only $2,000 had been collected as late as September 1868. At that time, the local voted to raise the full amount, which necessitated two assessments of $10 each upon all members.[63] It is unclear if the full amount was ever raised, but the experience of the plasterers suggests the difficulty of collecting such assessments. By the end of July, the plasterers' union of New York City had pledged $6,000 to the bricklayers, but they had contributed only $4,000—all from their treasury. The plasterers then promised to tax their members $2 per week to provide $1,800 per week for the duration of the strike. However, the assessment produced only $750 in additional funds.[64]

Finally, in evaluating the financial support received by the bricklayers, one must consider their own resources and the progress of the strike. The bricklayers had their own funds,[65] which were used so fully that the locals were unable to pay their per capita tax to the national union the following year.[66] Moreover, the actual number of men to be supported by strike benefits was reduced to a minimum by those who found work out of town as well as the sizable number who were at work for employers who temporarily accepted the eight-hour system. The striking locals also assessed themselves. The largest local (No. 2) taxed each member at work 10 percent of his weekly wages. This could mean from $2.50 to $3.00 for a fully employed worker. In late August, this tax was changed to a flat $2.00 per week.[67] This tax, even if not fully collected, significantly aided in meeting the needs of the strike fund.

In sum, the real restraints upon unity among workers in the 1860s were not dissolved by even so important an event as the bricklayers' strike. The strike was truly regarded as a test case for the viability of eight hours, and the support received by the strikers was greater than in any other strike in New York City during this period; but clearly such support was proportionate to the concrete effect of the strike upon the interests of the workers involved—in particular the likelihood that the success or failure of the strike would affect the hours situation in a particular local.

The bricklayers also sought to break the resistance of the employers by actions unrelated to the financial strength of the striking unions. One device for convincing employers to adopt eight hours was to increase productivity in the shorter day. Thus the employers' association learned in late July that bricklayers employed at eight hours were laying 1,800 bricks per day instead of the 1,000 figure for a ten-hour-day. However, a leader of the association regarded this increase in productivity as purely a tactic: should the bricklayers win the shorter day, he believed they would then adjust the amount of work to be done as they pleased.[68]

The strike committee also sought to employ some of the idle bricklayers by soliciting work itself under the eight-hour system. By the end of July, the strike committee claimed to have twenty-five contracts worth $300,000. The work was to be done primarily by small cooperative groups of bricklayers, although some single-person units were involved. As the strike dragged into August, a formal cooperative building society was organized by the three striking unions. An initial capital fund of $20,000 was proposed, with shares at $10 each to be offered to the bricklayers "and others willing to subscribe." Those willing to subscribe were few, and by September 1, only 64 shares had been sold. The number reached 100 by mid-September. Although the society organized and elected trustees, by November only 661 shares had been sold.[69] Considering the wide discussion of producers' cooperation in the 1860s, it is not unexpected that the bricklayers should turn to this device. However, in this case, it was clearly related to the exigencies of the strike, and not to any great commitment to the idea among the bricklayers of New York City. Thus it is no surprise that it failed.

The bricklayers also requested the support of their fellow unionists in New York City through sympathetic trade action. As early as June 26, a joint committee of plasterers and bricklayers was established to try to avoid disputes over jobs. However, the plasterers' union refused to order its members to stop work on projects that employed bricklayers at ten hours. The union informed the bricklayers that it had no rule binding its members not to work with nonunion craftsmen in other trades.[70] Thus despite the strong support offered by the plasterers, the limits were clear: they were not prepared to engage in a sympathy strike to support the bricklayers. In addition, the plasterers had their own complaints. It was claimed that bricklayers were doing plastering at two nonunion sites.[71]

The difficulties in cooperation also can be seen in the action of the laborers' union. This union viewed the strike as an opportunity for its unskilled membership to secure eight hours as well. Thus, in early July, the laborers' union refused to work with bricklayers who were breaking the strike by accepting ten hours.[72] This action soon turned into a strike by the laborers themselves for eight hours. However, a dispute then developed with the bricklayers because the laborers refused to offer a reduction in wages along with the demand for the shorter day. The bricklayers claimed such an approach prolonged the strike. The more poorly paid laborers were unprepared to accept eight hours if it meant a further diminution of their wages. Uneasy cooperation between the two unions continued into August.[73] Despite these problems with the plasterers and laborers, which were common enough even in normal times, the record reveals a high degree of cooperation among trade unions during the period of the strike.

Despite the wide range of support from other trade unions and the labor movement in general; despite the bricklayers' own considerable resources; and despite splits in the ranks of the employers, with the result that a significant number of bricklayers secured eight hours during the strike, the unions did not achieve their objective. A number of employers gave in to the demand for eight hours almost immediately.[74] However, the employers' association claimed that many of these contractors were obliged to concede the workers' demand in order to avoid default on their existing projects.[75] Once the ongoing project was completed, eight hours might not be retained. Throughout the strike, the claims of how many workers were employed at eight or ten hours varied widely depending upon whether the unions or the employers were supplying the numbers. At the end of August, the strike committee reported that 1,773 men were working eight hours, 955 were employed ten hours, and 174 were idle. Less than two weeks later, the *Workingman's Advocate* cited 1,230 bricklayers at work eight hours, 780 employed for ten hours, and 203 idle. In November, Local No. 2 reported 1,030 of its members at work eight hours, 511 on the ten-hour day, and 76 idle.[76] Thus, the unions maintained that a majority of the workers had gained the eight-hour day. Employers strongly contested these figures. Moreover, defections had been significant enough that two of the locals offered amnesty to members who had accepted ten hours and thus were strikebreakers.[77]

The employers' association had actively recruited strikebreakers from other areas, and by the end of August, it claimed that the strike was lost since employers had all the bricklayers they needed for ten hours.[78] The employers could argue the strike was thereby a failure, but the unions could point to the large number of bricklayers working eight hours. This situation allowed for a serious effort at a compromise settlement in mid-August 1868. The unions offered to permit employers an unlimited number of apprentices (a long-standing issue), and to allow employers to work on jobs without belonging to the union, in exchange for the eight-hour day. Samuel Gaul, president of Local No. 2, also claimed that had the employers conceded eight hours initially, the unions would have accepted $4 per day. This would have been a 20 percent reduction in wages to offset the 20 percent reduction in hours. The employers rejected the compromise, most probably because they believed that the strike was failing.[79] Thus the stoppage continued through the rest of the peak construction season without a general agreement for the eight-hour day, and without a formal end of the strike by the unions.

In evaluating the results of the strike, one must consider both the short-run situation and the broader implications. Clearly a significant number of workers gained eight hours and held it through 1868, although the pressure to return to the ten-hour day was strong.[80] Yet in December 1868, the unions already were demanding the eight-hour day for 1869, and the employers were preparing to oppose.[81] Thus the issue was still unsettled. However, the struggle of 1868 had exhausted both parties, and there were only discussions on the question of hours in 1869, not a strike. These negotiations did not produce eight hours, and by June 1869 it was claimed that most bricklayers were working ten hours once more.[82] In 1872, the bricklayers were among the first trade unions to secure eight hours in the great wave of strikes. Again the shorter day was ultimately lost. Thus despite the employment of a large number of bricklayers for eight hours during the strike of 1868, the shorter day did not become a permanent part of the working conditions in the trade.

It is not surprising that those bricklayers who initially won the shorter day had to concede their gain. As long as ten hours continued in the same local market, the competitive pressures on employers who worked only eight hours were severe, especially since the wage concession by the unions in June 1868 was proportionately less than the reduction in hours. Also the differential in wages led some workers to abandon eight hours to secure the higher wages available for ten hours. In some cases, employers offered as much as $5.50 per day (or $1.00 per day above the wage figure set by the unions for eight hours) as an inducement for bricklayers to abandon the strike.

Beyond the short-run considerations lay the broader implications of the strike—which had raised it above the level of an ordinary trade dispute. The bricklayers' strike was a test of the value of the eight-hour laws and a reaffirmation of the basic importance of the shorter day. If well-organized, skilled craftsmen in New York City, supported by the local trade unions and the labor movement in general, buttressed by the eight-hour law of the state, and confronted by employers who were anxious to continue work on the many building projects in progress, could not win eight hours, then the outlook for less powerful groups of workers seemed dim. A victory by the bricklayers might have sparked a wave of strikes in New York City and elsewhere, much like those of 1872. Victory would have sustained the movement for eight hours, and it would have suggested that success was possible.

John Fortune, president of the Operative Plasterers of North America, commented on the bricklayers' strike at his union's convention in 1869. Although he believed that every effort for eight hours would succeed eventually, he conceded that "I have generally heard it rumored that the movement ended only in ruin and disaster."[83] The failure of the brick-layers' strike discouraged other trade unions from taking similar action, and the emphasis in New York City shifted back to political action—a tactic that accomplished little.[84] Nationwide, the eight-hour movement lost momentum after 1868 until the wave of strikes in New York City in 1872 revived it briefly.

The eight-hour day was a major demand of the labor movement in the 1860s, but there was insufficient strength to win it. Political action produced laws that were statements of encouragement more than enforceable statutes. The key to success lay in action by trade unions, and the failure of crucial strikes, such as that of the bricklayers, held back action by most unions. The eight-hour day had to await a later generation. In the 1880s and 1890s, the strongest unions, primarily locals in the construction trades, secured the eight-hour day as well as the half-day on Saturday. In the early twentieth century, shorter hours spread slowly through the work force. However, by 1929, only 45 percent of the wage earners in manufacturing worked forty-eight hours or less for a six-day week.[85] Eight hours, and the five-day week, became standard in the depression of the 1930s, through a combination of collective agreements and legislation. Thus the eight-hour day has become a general condition of employment only in our own times.

NOTES

1. On the eight-hour movement in the 1860s, see David Montgomery, *Beyond Equality: Labor and the Radical Republicans, 1862-1872* (New York, 1967), chs. 6 and 8; John Commons et al., *History of Labor in the United States* (New York, 1918), vol. 2, ch. 4; Jonathan Grossman, *William Sylvis, Pioneer of American Labor: A Study of the American Labor Movement During the Era of the Civil War* (New York, 1945), pp. 129-32, 238-47. On Ira Steward, see Irwin Yellowitz, *Industrialization and the American Labor Movement, 1850-1900* (Port Washington, N.Y., 1977), pp. 15-20 and passim; Montgomery, *Beyond Equality*, pp. 249-60; Dorothy Douglas, "Ira Steward on Consumption and Unemployment," *Journal of Political Economy*, 40 (August 1932): 532-43.
2. *Reports of Commissioners on the Hours of Labor* (Massachusetts House Document No. 44, Boston, 1867), pp. 71-75. Also see Charles McLean's report to the convention of the Plasterers' International Union in 1868, *Workingman's Advocate*, July 11, 1868, p. 2.
3. C. W. Gibson, *Report to the Officers and Members of the National Labor Union* as found in Wisconsin State Historical Society, Labor Collection, 13A, Box 2. For other examples, see the National Labor Union, *Proceedings*, 1868, p. 34; President William Sylvis to the convention of the Iron Molders' International Union in 1864, *Fincher's Trades' Review*, January 16, 1864, p. 28; National Typographical Union, *Proceedings*, 1865, pp. 46-47; Interna-

tional Workingmen's Associations Proceedings, 1872, p. 4, typescript, Wisconsin State Historical Society, Labor Collection, 1A, Box 1.

4. John Fortune of the Plasterers' Union of New York City, *New York Sun,* August 13, 1868, p. 1; William Jessup, a prominent leader in the central labor organizations of New York City and New York State, *New York World,* April 8, 1872, p. 1. On this point, see Sam B. Warner Jr., *Streetcar Suburbs: The Process of Growth in Boston, 1870-1900* (Cambridge, 1962).

5. For Whaley's statement, see *Welcome Workman,* October 26, 1867, p. 5. For a fine example of the education theme, see the statement by A. M. Winn in Mechanics State Council [California] *Constitution and By-Laws with Names of Associations and Delegates: A Condensed History of the Eight-Hour Movement in California* . . . (1868), p. 4. On office holding, see the "Address to the Workingmen of America," issued by the National Eight Hour Association (Philadelphia, n.d.), found in the Union Cooperative Association Papers, Wisconsin State Historical Society.

6. *Fincher's Trades' Review,* March 26, 1864, p. 66.

7. Ibid., June 27, 1863, p. 14. Also see W. H. Gudgeon, president of the Cincinnati Trades Assembly, ibid., May 13, 1865, p. 95.

8. Lawrence Costello, "The New York City Labor Movement, 1861-1873," Ph.D. dissertation, Columbia University, 1967, pp. 300-311.

9. *Fincher's Trades' Review,* January 16, 1864, p. 28.

10. Letter from "Faust," ibid., February 20, 1864, p. 47. Also see the statement by the president of the plumbers' union of New York City, ibid., March 4, 1865, p. 54; letter from "W.S.R.," ibid., August 5, 1865, p. 77.

11. For examples, see National Eight Hour Association, "Address to Workingmen"; letter from "One of the Workers," *New York Sun,* June 6, 1868, p. 2; letter from "A Seeker after Truth," *Workingman's Advocate,* June 20, 1868, p. 2; delegate George Cook, Bricklayers' National Union convention, ibid., February 20, 1869, p. 1; Massachusetts Bureau of Labor Statistics, *Fourth Annual Report,* 1873, p. 253.

12. *Workingman's Advocate,* July 30, 1870, p. 3.

13. Ibid., August 5, 1871, p. 3.

14. *New York Tribune,* May 28, 1872, p. 8.

15. For use of this argument by a nonlabor source, see the report of the speech by George A. Bandreth to the New York state assembly, which was considering an eight-hour law. *Workingman's Advocate,* April 21, 1866, p. 1.

16. *New York Sun,* June 23, 1868, p. 2; *New York Tribune,* letter to the editor, June 30, 1868, p. 2.

17. *Fincher's Trades' Review,* April 22, 1865, p. 83.

18. Ira Steward Papers, Wisconsin State Historical Society, Box 3, untitled essay, pp. 6-7; Massachusetts Bureau of Labor Statistics, *Second Annual Report,* 1871, pp. 585, 591-92.

19. *Fincher's Trades' Review,* June 3, 1865, p. 4.

20. Ibid., June 24, 1865, p. 29; September 2, 1865, p. 107; *Workingman's Advocate,* May 16, 1868, p. 2; April 10, 1869, p. 2; July 1, 1871, p. 2; American Workman, June 12, 1869, p. 16, typescript, Wisconsin State Historical Society, Labor Collection 11A, Box A. At its convention in 1867, the Cigar Makers' International Union supported the campaign for eight hours. However, the union proposed no concrete action of its own, and it hoped that the efforts "will be successful without reduction of wages." Cigar Makers' International Union, *Proceedings,* 1867, p. 45.

21. On the carpenters and joiners, see *Workingman's Advocate,* September 19, 1868, p. 4. Also see the speech by L. C. Hughes to the convention of the Machinists' and Blacksmiths' Union in the *Machinists' and Blacksmiths' International Journal,* 8 (December 1870): 46.

22. Costello, "New York City Labor Movement," pp. 65, 577.

23. *Workingman's Advocate,* August 18, 1866, p. 2. Cameron also was involved in the activities of the National Labor Union. On the general issue of politics and trade union action within the labor movement of the 1860s, see the contrasting views of Gerald Grob, *Workers and Utopia: A Study of Ideological Conflict in the American Labor Movement, 1865-1900* (Evanston, Ill., 1961), chs. 1, 2, and 10, and Montgomery, *Beyond Equality,* passim.

24. *Workingman's Advocate,* July 28, 1866, p. 4.

25. Costello, "New York City Labor Movement," pp. 339–46 and table of strikes, pp. 558–76.

26. Statement in the *New York Sun* as found in the *Workingman's Advocate,* May 12, 1866, p. 1.

27. On the strike, see the *Workingman's Advocate* for the period May 12–July 14, 1866; on financial support by other workers, see the *New York Herald,* May 16, 20, June 16, 1866. The house painters also lost their strike for eight hours.

28. *New York Sun,* June 15, 1866, p. 2.

29. On the campaign for the eight-hour law, see James C. Mohr, *The Radical Republicans and Reform in New York during Reconstruction* (Ithaca, N.Y., 1973), pp. 120-39.

30. For complaints about the weaknesses of the eight-hour laws passed in New York and Pennsylvania, see the letters in the *Workingman's Advocate,* May 30, 1868, p. 2; June 6, 1868, p. 2; August 22, 1868, p. 2.

31. Montgomery, *Beyond Equality,* pp. 324-26; Costello, "New York City Labor Movement," pp. 349-50.

32. Costello, "New York City Labor Movement," p. 356. Employers had used the conspiracy suit against the bricklayers in 1868; ibid., pp. 264-69.

33. Montgomery, *Beyond Equality,* pp. 326-32; Costello, "New York City Labor Movement," pp. 357-76.

34. National Typographical Union, *Proceedings,* 1865, pp. 46-47.

35. *Fincher's Trades' Review,* January 28, 1865, p. 34.

36. *Workingman's Advocate,* July 11, 1868, p. 2.

37. See Carpenters' and Joiners' National Union of the United States of America, *Proceedings,* 1865, pp. 11, 27, and president Thomas Shaw, ibid., 1867, pp. 8-9.

38. Costello, "New York City Labor Movement," is the best source on this subject. On the frequency and success of strikes, see p. 577. For the positive view of strikes enunciated by local trade union leaders, see p. 315. On the organization of the bricklayers, see Appendix II, table 10. On the membership and financial strength of the bricklayers' locals, see *New York Times,* June 23, 1868, p. 5; *New York Tribune,* June 23, 1868, p. 5; July 29, 1868, p. 8; *New York Sun,* July 30, 1868, p. 1. Compare the situation in the plasterers' union, which had secured eight hours in 1867, in *New York Sun,* July 1, 1868, p. 1. On the initiation fees, see Costello, pp. 92-93. On conditions in the construction industry, see p. 29. On the number and continuity of trade unions, see ch. 3 and p. 580. Five local unions survived the period 1861-73. Thirty-eight operated for more than ten years, and forty-seven lasted for a seven- to nine-year period.

39. Bricklayers' National Union, *Proceedings,* 1868, pp. 20, 49-51.

40. Harry Bates, *Bricklayers' Century of Craftsmanship: A History of the Bricklayers, Masons and Plasterers' International Union of America* (Washington, D.C., 1955), pp. 26-29.

41. Bricklayers' National Union, *Proceedings,* 1868, pp. 49-52, 56-59.

42. *New York Evening Telegram,* June 13, 1868, p. 4.

43. *New York Sun,* July 17, 1868, p. 3; July 27, 1868, p. 3; July 31, 1868, p. 1; August 3, 1868, p. 3.

44. *New York Evening Telegram,* June 19, 1868, p. 3.

45. *New York Times,* June 25, 1868, p. 2.

46. *New York Sun,* June 23, 1868, p. 2; June 27, 1868, pp. 2, 3; *New York Tribune,* June 30, 1868, p. 2.
47. *Workingman's Advocate,* August 22, 1868, p. 2.
48. *New York Sun,* August 13, 1868, p. 1; *New York Tribune,* August 13, 1868, p. 8. On efforts by the labor movement in Chicago to enforce Illinois's eight-hour law in 1867, see Montgomery, *Beyond Equality,* pp. 306-11. For efforts to make the law of 1867 in New York effective, see pp. 324-26.
49. For the Council session, see *Workingman's Advocate,* August 22, 1868, p. 4. For the platform of 1866, see John Commons et al., *A Documentary History of American Industrial Society,* 10 vols. (Cleveland, 1910), 9:140, and also 9:130-32, 155-56. On the debate in 1868, see pp. 206-8. For Cameron's evaluation, see *Workingman's Advocate,* November 14, 1868, p. 2.
50. *New York Sun,* June 23, 1868, p. 2; June 25, 1868, p. 3.
51. Ibid., July 13, 1868, p. 3.
52. Ibid., September 2, 1868, p. 1.
53. Ibid., September 3, 1868, p. 1; *New York Evening Telegram,* September 24, 1868, p. 4.
54. Strike benefits were set originally at $12 per week for single members of locals Nos. 2 and 12, and $15 for members of Local No. 4. *New York Sun,* July 13, 1868, p. 3. The benefit of $12 was reduced to $7 in late July. *New York Tribune,* July 24, 1868, p. 8. One should compare these benefits to the wage of $5 per day earned before the strike.
55. Costello, "New York City Labor Movement," p. 95.
56. *New York Sun,* July 30, 1868, p. 1; *New York Evening Telegram,* November 13, 1868, p. 4.
57. *Workingman's Advocate,* August 1, 1868, p. 2.
58. Bates, *Bricklayers' History,* pp. 29-30.
59. *New York Sun,* August 27, 1868, p. 3; September 11, 1868, p. 3; *New York Evening Telegram,* September 11, 1868, p. 4.
60. For the debate, see *Workingman's Advocate,* February 20, 1869, p. 1. Even when an assessment was voted, it was not necessarily paid. An assessment had been approved by the Bricklayers' National Union in 1868 to support those leaders of the strike in New York City who had been convicted in the conspiracy case that grew out of the stoppage. However, only nineteen of the forty-seven locals met their assessment. See the *Workingman's Advocate,* January 22, 1870, p. 1.
61. On the financial aid from the plasterers, see *New York Sun,* June 29, 1868, p. 3; July 8, 1868, p. 2; July 30, 1868, p. 1.
62. Ibid., June 30, 1868, p. 2; July 18, 1868, p. 3; July 30, 1868, p. 1.
63. *New York Evening Telegram,* September 12, 1868, p. 4; September 14, 1868, p. 4.
64. *New York Tribune,* July 30, 1868, p. 8; *New York Sun,* October 21, 1868, p. 1. The $750 was contributed to the strike fund in early September. See *New York Sun,* September 5, 1868, p. 3.
65. Estimates of the treasuries of the locals, before the strike, varied from $6,000 to $10,000. See *New York Times,* June 23, 1868, p. 5, and *New York Sun,* July 30, 1868, p. 1. Local No. 2, the largest local on strike, reported that receipts from internal sources for the period March 19 to September 18, 1868, had been $4,016.50 despite the strike. *New York Sun,* September 18, 1868, p. 1.
66. Bates, *Bricklayers' History,* p. 36.
67. *New York Sun,* August 21, 1868, p. 1.
68. Ibid., July 21, 1868, p. 3.
69. Ibid., July 27, 1868, p. 3; July 30, 1868, p. 1; August 15, 1868, p. 1; September 1, 1868, p. 1; September 16, 1868, p. 1; *New York Evening Telegram,* October 3, 1868, p. 4; November 7, 1868, p. 4; November 11, 1868, p. 1.

70. *New York Sun,* June 26, 1868, p. 1; August 26, 1868, p. 1.
71. Ibid., August 7, 1868, p. 1; August 28, 1868, p. 1.
72. *New York World,* July 11, 1868, p. 2; *New York Evening Telegram,* July 14, 1868, p. 4.
73. *New York Sun,* July 24, 1868, p. 3; *New York Evening Telegram,* July 31, 1868, p. 1; August 11, 1868, p. 4.
74. *New York World,* June 23, 1868, p. 5.
75. *New York Sun,* July 4, 1868, p. 2; August 1, 1868, p. 3.
76. For the figures cited, see ibid., September 1, 1868, p. 1; *Workingman's Advocate,* September 12, 1868, p. 2; *New York Evening Telegram,* November 13, 1868, p. 4. Also see the *New York Sun,* August 22, 1868, p. 3.
77. *New York Sun,* August 27, 1868, p. 3; August 28, 1868, p. 1.
78. *New York Tribune,* August 22, 1868, p. 5; August 29, 1868, p. 5; *Workingman's Advocate,* September 19, 1868, p. 2.
79. *New York Sun,* August 11, 1868, p. 1; August 15, 1868, p. 1; August 18, 1868, p. 3.
80. *New York Evening Telegram,* October 16, 1868, p. 4; Costello, "New York City Labor Movement," p. 355.
81. *New York Sun,* December 18, 1868, p. 1.
82. Ibid., February 18, 1869, p. 1; March 4, 1869, p. 1; Costello, "New York City Labor Movement," p. 355.
83. *Workingman's Advocate,* July 24, 1869, p. 2.
84. Costello, "New York City Labor Movement," p. 356.
85. Irving Bernstein, *The Lean Years: A History of the American Worker, 1920–1933* (1960; Baltimore, 1966), p. 476.

MARK D. HIRSCH

6

RICHARD CROKER: AN INTERIM REPORT ON THE EARLY CAREER OF A "BOSS" OF TAMMANY HALL

I

When Urban C. Lehner wrote in May 1975[1] that the "classic political boss is facing, some say, [a] classic last hurrah," it may have been a premature, if not overoptimistic, prediction. Lehner was referring specifically to Peter J. Camiel, chairman of the Philadelphia Democratic City Committee, who was then feuding with Mayor Frank L. Rizzo. Camiel was further described as "one of a dying breed—the big-city 'boss' whose control over a political machine can make or break candidates for public office, influence key city and state legislation and even give him clout in national party councils."

Belying the "classic last hurrah," however, are (at this time of writing) Mayor Rizzo himself, and other present or past mayors like Chicago's recently deceased Richard J. Daley,[2] Albany's Erastus Corning II, San Francisco's Joseph L. Alioto, Detroit's Coleman A. Young, and numerous other city "bosses," either holding public office or holding court in party headquarters, district clubs, or their homes. It is true, however, that current political theory stresses that present-day city bosses are more likely to be officeholders, deriving their powers from office, than *non*officeholders, crouching behind the seats of authority and manipulating their occupants.[3] But whether as Warwicks and Richelieus or as officeholders, whether as mayors or as holders of higher or less exalted office (or as their new suburban counterparts), urban bosses dominating their political machines through highly trained, loyal, partisan infrastructures are no *dying breed.* Where circumstances permit or favor, they rise and still flourish. They may be relatively diminished in number, and their inner cities decaying at the core from overwhelming, different, and ever-more-complex problems than in past times, but these durable masters of power are a hardy lot. They grip their reins of authority and positions of influence grimly. There is no inclination to yield the dispensation of partisan favors and other largess after self-consideration and presumed sublimation of the party's welfare have taken place, but always on a calculated *quid pro quo* basis. The big city may be described as dying, but the big-city political boss or powerful political leader shows remarkable vitality in structuring advantageous or rationalized budgets and in orchestrating patronage, nominations and election campaigns.[4]

Lehner additionally observed that investigations of political corruption in Philadelphia were "as much a part of life here as political corruption itself; there is always at least one inquiry going on." Indeed, he alleged, the subject of his remarks had been called before more than one grand jury but never indicted!

What makes the whole question of any last hurrahs for city bosses so fascinating is that—by rolling back time by ninety years or less—all of the above facts, comments, and observations could have just as easily applied at one time or another to the career of Richard Croker, "Boss" of Tammany Hall from 1886 to 1902. That the connective linear descent of power and decision making both before and after Croker is so long attests to that vitality. Tammany, the recognized regular Democratic political organization in New York City and County, had shortly after mid-nineteenth century been dragged away from its earlier character and objectives by ruthless leaders like Fernando Wood and William Marcy ("Boss") Tweed. The latter is usually, and deservedly, thought of as the apogee of municipal graft and corruption, of personal thievery from the public till, and of an unrestrained evil political partisanship through the creation and operation of his infamous "Tweed Ring"—a personal conspiratorial organization designed to do his will—and its ugly practices. But if Tweed has fastened down his claim to this eternal damnation as the prototype, then Richard Croker is perhaps the closest archtype in Tammany's history.

Croker combined enough of Tweed's larcenous operations and un-scrupulousness with John Kelly's (Kelly was chieftain of Tammany between Tweed and Croker) tight organization and iron discipline, adding some contributions of his own, to make him singular in his own right.

The result of all these influences and forces was to mould him into a formidable political boss in the grand manner, master of his party and his city, and determined to block reform of the political process at any point and any cost.

Lyle W. Dorsett has described succinctly the breeding ground and seedtime for the style of urban bossism that produced and nourished a Croker. "The industrial revolution," he writes,[5]

destroyed the pre-industrial order and left in its wake burgeoning cities composed of numerous new interest groups. Cities changed so drastically during the industrial boom that old power structures were rendered impotent. The extent of urban change in the last half of the nineteenth century can be seen in the population explosion. To cite only one decade: Manhattan in 1880 had 1,911,692 people but in 1890 this figure was over 2,500,000.

And this was the decade that witnessed Croker's rise to power. Dorsett further reminds us of the obvious. Part of this growth was owing to tremendous immigration after the Civil War, with the result that New York City by 1890 had a population that was four-fifths foreign-born or of foreign parentage. Like many other political scientists, however, his analysis is ambivalent. On the one hand the boss and his machine are complimented for bringing order and agreement out of strife and chaos through organization and power brokerage; on the other, "The new political structure . . . was expensive. It cost the taxpayers hundreds of thousands of dollars in graft and inefficiency." But Dorsett proceeds again to excuse the machine because "it is doubtful if any alternative existed in most major cities."

Both sides of Dorsett's coin are valid. The critical question becomes: At what point does a machine become *too* evil, too pervasively corrupt and morally destructive to remain tolerable and forgivable? Admitting all the new problems commonly besetting all the growing urban enclaves and the shrewdness of the boss in discerning a new clientele in the manual laborer, the factory hand, the immigrant, the clerk, the humble public servant, and the impoverished slum dweller generally, there were machine leaders running the entire gamut of the political spectrum from vicious to reasonably beneficent. Political parties, leaders, and even "club houses" —especially in times before social welfare legislation—can have an important and useful function in organizing and mounting political campaigns in a democratic society, in giving direction to an urban administration, and when supportive and compassionate toward those who are poor or inarticulate, seeking a spokesman, or in need of a defender. Croker and his Tammany frequently performed some of these functions. In these new political wavelengths, however, Croker's type of bossism took on much too dark a hue. The benefits he may have conferred incidentally were outweighed by the toll he in turn exacted from New York.

A nagging thought intrudes itself: Do the boss and his political machine represent a *modern* counterpart and rationale for Thomas Hobbes's theory of indirect government?[6] Men consent to be governed by a created boss— the new sovereign—whose assumption of authority permits escape from political turmoil and controversy. In 1894, in Croker's heyday, David MacGregor Means stressed that same concept, although blaming men of substance and affairs more than "the common people" for creating the boss because of their preoccupation "in necessary work," having little time

to consult as to the manner after which, or the men by whom, they desire to be governed; moreover their numbers are so great that they cannot know one another, and it is impossible for them all, or for any great part of them, to meet together in one place for deliberation. Therefore they cannot agree upon any one particular man for their ruler, for no man is known to all of them; nor can they determine upon any plan whereby they will be governed.

The ordinary citizenry, in Means's cynical view, were more interested in the egalitarian exercise of the vote than in "the nature of the laws or the character of their rulers." And so enter secretly the "sharp-sighted men" into the picture.[7] The Richard Crokers take over—but few took over as well as he.

If it is conceded that Croker left an indelible imprint upon the city's politics and history and that his methods were quickly reflected in Tammany's own frequently illicit and publicly damaging policies—so much so that the image of the man and the image of the organization superimposed into a single sharp focus—then it would be profitable to examine at least his early life and rise to power. So, while Croker was no monster or depraved character, his venality, greed, and lust for power make this the story (truncated here to reach no further than the Fassett Investigation of 1890) of a checkered career, of a man who literally bullied his way into power and for sixteen years ruled his party like a private fiefdom without holding major public office after 1890, let alone practicing a profession or an open, outside business or a career!

II

Richard Croker was born on either November 23 or 24, 1843, in Black Rock or Cloghnakilty (or Clonakilty, at the head of Clonakilty Bay, opening onto the Atlantic), in County Cork, Ireland. The records are dim or nonexistent, the data frequently contradictory.[8] Croker's father was Eyre Coote Croker, a descendant of an English soldier who had come over into Ireland with Cromwell's invading army. His mother (Christian name unknown) was a member of a Scottish family named Wellstead that had also immigrated, but just when is not known.

Separating myth from fact, romantic fabrication from reality, and ego-exercise from mundane truth becomes a frustrating task as one dips ever farther back into the murky past of Croker's ancestry. The Croker lineage claimed without genealogical evidence a governor of Bermuda, a member of Parliament, and a British army major. Eyre Coote himself was subsequently said to be a graduate of Trinity College in Dublin, a veterinary surgeon, a civil engineer, a captain under General Daniel E. Sickles during the Civil War, a British army officer—or, to temper these and leaven fantasy, a blacksmith, a squatter, or a general purchasing agent for the Harlem Railroad.

By Eyre Coote's time, improvidence, poverty and hard times overtook and readied the family to leave Ireland for the young country of golden promise and fresh opportunity. The Crokers set sail aboard the *Henry Clay* with their brood of nine children—including Richard, aged three— and arrived in New York sometime in the autumn of 1846.

As with so many other immigrant families, high hopes gave way to disillusionment and harsh reality. The elder Croker found it difficult to get steady employment, let alone a suitable position as a veterinarian. The family quickly moved from its first hovel in the congested slums of lower Manhattan into the "Shantytown" area of squatters in what is presently Central Park; then, on to Cincinnati for an undetermined interlude; a return to New York and settlement at Madison Avenue and East Twenty-fourth Street, on the site of the original Madison Square Garden; and, still later, on Twenty-eighth Street near Third Avenue.[9]

Family fortunes improved. The father, after some four years, enjoyed regular employment, first as a stableman and later as an assistant veterinarian for a street horsecar line. Young Richard was now able to attend primary school on Madison and East Twenty-sixth Street and later grammar school on East Twenty-seventh Street, but his schooling was said to have been anywhere between two or three and seven years, of a rudimentary nature, and anything but distinguished. Reading was especially a chore for him, and he apparently bowed out at age twelve or thirteen. Very powerful and athletic, although on the short side, Richard was decidedly more partial to sports and outdoor life than to the confinement of the classroom.[10]

At age thirteen Croker was apprenticed as a machinist in the Harlem Railroad machine shops for about six years, moved on about 1862 to the job of machinist in a Brooklyn marine shop for six or seven months,[11] and next took a common road in progressing up the political ladder (as had "Boss" Tweed), and joined the city's volunteer fire department as engine stoker on the first steam fire engine in New York. Subsequently he rose to foreman of Engine Company No. 28.[12]

More conducive to Croker's political ascent than this succession of jobs were his physical prowess and sleazy youthful activities. As a teenager he had become a member of a predatory neighborhood gang of juvenile hoodlums known as the Fourth Avenue Tunnel Gang.[13] His hamlike fists could have brought him prominence as a professional boxer, but he used them instead to batter down any opposition both within and outside the gang. His exploits made him a neighborhood celebrity and brought him to the attention of the local Tammany leadership, headed by Sheriff James O'Brien, an important lieutenant of Tweed's. In today's jargon, Croker became an enforcer. After election in 1865, William H. Lyman, Democratic candidate for constable in Greenpoint, admitted: "Richard Croker voted for me seventeen times in one day and he was at the head of a gang of repeaters that day."[14] In 1868, on the corner of Thirty-second Street and Second Avenue, he and his gang knocked Christopher Pullman, a leading Republican politician, unconscious and allegedly injured him for life.[15] On October 13, 1868, the *New York Tribune*, in reporting on fraudulent Democratic voters and repeaters imported into Philadelphia for the Pennsylvania state elections the following day, stated:[16]

. . . and a number of other organized bands of roughs left this classic locality [New York], and, last but not least, were 150 Metropolitan bandits, under the notorious Dick Croker, all well armed and spoiling for a fight. They hailed from the Twenty-first Ward [O'Brien's district].

As a reward for these feats, Croker prospered in O'Brien's orbit. He also enjoyed the useful friendship of Tweed and other members of the Ring. In 1867 Croker was appointed attendant in notorious (later impeached) state Supreme Court Judge George G. Barnard's court at a salary of $1,200 per annum—actually a sinecure, since he never seemed to appear for the sessions. The following year he ran successfully for alderman from the Eighteenth District and was reelected in 1869, only to be legislated out of office after some five months by the new "Tweed Charter" of 1870, a state charter achieved through bribery and fraud that neutralized the interference of the state in local affairs, virtually turned over the city to the Ring, and provided for a new but weaker Board of Aldermen.[17]

Tweed, by this coup, was able as well to blunt a dangerous palace rebellion by Sheriff O'Brien resulting from a falling out over the division of spoils. O'Brien, rebuffed in his efforts for a greater share and ousted as sheriff, had with the help of other hungry dissidents created a rival Democratic, spurious-reform faction in the city, the Young Democracy, earlier in 1870.[18] Tagging along after his padrone was Richard Croker. Indeed, together with eight other anti-Tweed aldermen, Croker had already signed an unlawful agreement on March 20, 1870, that they would not vote for the confirmation of any appointee created under the city charter, or any laws of the state, or adopt any ordinance or any resolution affecting city or county government without consulting certain anti-Tweed leaders "and first obtaining their consent"![19] And then Tweed in vengeance had turned mass executioner. No machine, especially one as corrupt and ugly as the Tweed Ring, could long survive without stern discipline and severe retribution for disloyalty.

Croker's actions for the next year or two are not easy to follow, but a certain partisan pattern habitual to machine politics possibly points the way to untanglement. Undoubtedly he smarted from the loss of his prestigious aldermanic seat, which had brought him $4,000 a year. He now apparently got two jobs in 1870, either concurrently or one close upon the other. He became superintendent of market rents and fees in the Bureau of City Revenue, at $3,000 per annum.[20] Sometime after June 1870 he was also appointed a city marshal for the collection of arrears in personal taxes,[21] in the office of Comptroller Richard B. ("Slippery Dick")

Connolly, one of the four top Tweed Ring leaders. Either Croker realized the loneliness—to him, futility—and loss of a power base when standing on the outside looking in and had therefore made quiet peace with enough of the Tammany leaders to recapture some of his earlier recognition;[22] or, he may have acted as agent for the mercurial O'Brien in the latter's calculated plot to destroy Tweed.

The shifty sheriff had been successful himself in establishing some degree of *rapprochement* with Tweed after his abortive defection. We know that O'Brien had now borrowed at least a total of $36,000 from the boss between September 1869 and May 1871, included in which was a $12,000 thirty-day promissory note dated May 1, 1871, and therefore due for collection on the following June 1. But on June 3, O'Brien refused to pay. We also know that a few days earlier he had quietly provided Louis John Jennings, editor of the *New York Times,* with transcripts of Connolly's records, revealing a long digest of frauds, theft, and corruption by Tweed and his coconspirators. The *Times* began its historic disclosures of this damning evidence on July 8, 1871, and followed it up editorially and with additional incriminatory revelations on July 19 and 20. On July 22, the *Times* stepped up its courageous onslaught on the Ring with a chapter of figures from Connolly's books on its front page "revealing fraudulent warrants—illegally certified by the [Tweed-dominated] board of audit—paid out in 1869 and 1870 for repairs and furniture for the new courthouse. On July 24 and through weeks following, more jarring disclosures filled the *Times.*"[23] The newspaper now led the call for criminal prosecution. This was soon to come.

Now as to the *why* and the *who.* Why did O'Brien undertake this role of seeking and supplying undercover information? Surely revenge and unflagging ambition to lead Tammany and seek higher political office. Surely the desire to pose as a pious reformer in engineering the downfall of the Ring was to further that ambition. But just as surely, greed. With Tweed disposed of, the sheriff stood to gain through default anywhere from $12,000 to $35,000 (a considerable sum for the time) all in the same maneuver. An irresistible complex of motivations, each interlinked. As for the who, it becomes an exercise in tantalizing speculation that the strategically placed man who actually secured, or arranged to secure, the data that started the downfall of the most vicious political machine in American history was very possibly, if not most likely, its heir and the future autocrat of Tammany Hall—Richard Croker![24]

When the Ring was toppled through these welcome disclosures and attacks, James O'Brien's hopes soared. In the infighting that followed, however, both he and Samuel J. Tilden, as well as lesser Tammany hopefuls, ultimately lost out to "Honest John" Kelly, who succeeded Tweed as boss of the Wigwam. This time Richard Croker did not follow his defeated mentor out of the Hall. A career of small-time sniping against an all-powerful organization offered too unattractive an existence and too precarious a future to a young politician aspiring to the upper councils and he quickly fell in step behind John Kelly. As a result, O'Brien and he now became mortal enemies. Skillfully ingratiating himself into his new leader's confidence and thereby establishing himself again as a virtual protégé, Croker had high prospects once more.

In these political oscillations he became the bone of contention between Kelly, who was also sheriff at the time, and newly elected Republican Mayor William F. Havemeyer. Kelly nominated his new lieutenant for the important position of coroner in November 1873. Havemeyer properly opposed the nomination. Croker was absolutely unqualified, but he won election.[25] His new office paid him $15,000 in fees[26] and served merely as a rich source of patronage for Tammany.

Croker's victory positively infuriated the acerbic, elderly mayor, and his sharp attacks upon Kelly rapidly escalated. Their feud culminated in a spectacular libel suit brought by the boss in November 1874 in which Havemeyer seemingly had the better of it, providing us with some valuable information about Kelly's methods, but it was tragically terminated by the sudden death of the mayor on November 30.[27] The historical profession thus lost an opportunity to learn still more informative disclosures about Kelly and Tammany from Havemeyer's testimony.

At the very time that death extricated Kelly (although he was the plaintiff) from an unhappy position, it plagued his staunchest follower, Croker, and plunged him into one of the most dangerous crises of his life. While supposedly the august and prestigious coroner of New York County, in Tammany's scheme of things this did not excuse him from his house duties in the exercise of his conspicuous talents. On election day, November 3, 1874, while poll watching, intimidating, and containing the opposition, he and a band of his followers chanced upon a rival group in front of a polling place on East Thirty-fourth Street and Second Avenue, led by his implacable foe, now state senator, O'Brien, the anti-Tammany Apollo Hall candidate for congressman. Croker and O'Brien, and their supporters, exchanged insults, and a savage street brawl between the two statesmen and the others broke out. In the midst of the fracas a shot rang out; John McKenna, an O'Brienite, was struck in the head and fell dying. Before he expired, he accused Croker of firing the revolver.

O'Brien and his followers also swore at the inquest that Croker had killed McKenna, which Croker and his faction denied. Actually, the evidence pointed away from Croker, but although a coroner's jury (an ironic twist) cleared him and three followers, he was nevertheless indicted on November 17 for what the *New York Times* called "a political murder," committed to the Tombs, denied bail, and forced to undergo a four-day trial, December 8-12, for his life. The jury disagreed, six to six, and he was freed; but he was never cleared and remained deeply scarred and stigmatized in the community.[28]

III

Croker was one of four coroners in the city and county, *only one of whom was a physician!* Another was a lawyer turned editor; a third, Henry Woltman, was "a mere ward politician"; and, although Croker maintained to a state senate committee investigating several of the city and county departments of New York in 1876 that his occupation was twice an alderman and additionally, that he was "a machinist by trade," that Committee's report described him as no more than "a blacksmith by trade." There was no disgrace to blacksmithing, but his testimony was mocked as "a fair illustration of the progressive and enlightened views of duty entertained by that intelligent official, Richard Croker, coroner"! It was readily apparent how much schooling he had had.[29]

The Committee issued its report on March 15, 1876, and its conclusions on the coroners were positively devastating.[30] While too lengthy to detail here, some observations on Croker demand attention. His conception of his duties was a classic:

The duties of a coroner is to inquire how and in what manner in behalf of the dead, and in what way, and into all the circumstances connected with the person who may be dead; that is, that may be reported to the office as coroner's cases.[31]

The report noted that a J. J. McDonald was Croker's favorite juror. He had appeared in 118 inquest jury cases, but the year before he had also been sentenced to a year in the penitentiary for sexually assaulting the body of a dead woman in the morgue. Yet, Croker regarded him as a proper person to sit upon a coroner's jury as well as being "an unusually intelligent man." Croker could not even remember McDonald's first name.[32] The report concluded:

It is the belief of the Committee that no one of them [the coroners] could, in a private capacity, earn one-third the amount they receive for official services, which, when performed, are discharged in so incompetent, extravagant and illegal a manner, as to be wholly without benefit to the public.[33]

This was the first of the four state legislative investigations in which Richard Croker was to figure. While not the major target at this time, he was already singled out by it as demonstrating the curse of Tammany politics and partisan patronage.

Withal, Croker ultimately weathered the storm. Kelly and Tammany, as well as political allies on the fringes, stood by him staunchly in the McKenna tribulation. Some contributed to his legal expenses. Time was mainly on his side. There seems to be no evidence that he ever acted again as a marauding deputy. Kelly kept him close by, and it must have been intensely gratifying to them both when Croker—surviving the rebuke and escaping punishment or removal—was reelected coroner for a second three-year term on November 7, 1876.[34]

Nevertheless, Croker's fortunes rose and ebbed with Tammany's own progress. His term as coroner ended on January 1, 1880, and he was without a position. He still bore the ugly taint of the McKenna tragedy, and Kelly at the moment could give him little assistance. The boss had outraged the state democracy by his selfish, obstructive tactics. He had needlessly and stubbornly created a schism within it in 1879 that had caused the loss of the state election and the victory of Republican Governor Alonzo B. Cornell. A new reformist Democratic party, the New York County Democracy, was therefore organized in the city in 1880 to challenge and displace, if not destroy, Tammany. It was more fully structured and strengthened the following year.[35] As a result, with bleak prospects, Croker removed to White Plains, New York, commenced an ice business in 1880, and continued it until 1882 or 1883.[36]

In 1882, county Democracy nominee Franklin P. Edson was elected mayor, but with the support of Tammany in the interest of party harmony and to ensure concurrently the vital election of Grover Cleveland as governor of New York State. Part of the price the county Democracy had had to pay for this backing had been a grudging promise to divide the patronage that would come with victory.[37] One of the prized traditional plums to Tammany was a police justiceship, and Kelly promptly moved in to claim it as part of the bargain—for Croker. Edson, however, looked askance at this piece of arrogance. Croker was as little qualified to be a judge as he had been to be a coroner. The mayor would not accede unless Croker ran for some public office and was vindicated at the polls. Tammany then nominated Croker for alderman in 1883, and upon his election Kelly once again put his favorite forth for police justice. Edson apparently refused to lend himself to this travesty, nominated his fire commissioner, John J. Gorman, to be police justice and appointed Croker into the former's vacancy on November 15, 1883. When county Democrat Abram S. Hewitt became mayor in 1886, also with Tammany's support, he appointed Croker for the full term as fire commissioner.[38] Croker was on the rise again.

The year 1886 proved a momentous one for him. John Kelly had fallen victim to some degenerative disease, possibly cancer, had been ailing since November 1884, and toward the end was confined to his home. Among the heirs apparent was Croker. He had been tasting the heady draughts of the return from oblivion; now, by a queer quirk, he stood possibly a heart beat away from the threshold of power. He adopted the gambit of a determined assertion to leadership, elbowing aside any nascent competition, manipulating the sinking Kelly, and establishing his own succession as the putative order of things. He took advantage of his almost father-son, favored status in Kelly's eyes (there was even some facial resemblance between the two), visited his dying chief at home daily, and thereby deliberately gave the impression that he was receiving and carrying out orders and being groomed for the succession. When he would return from these pilgrimages, he would seclude himself in his office. By the time of Kelly's death on June 1, 1886, it was a foregone conclusion to most that Croker would be the next boss. The day after Kelly's funeral the district leaders, who had wanted an interim ruling committee, "were still squabbling over seniority when Richard Croker walked into Honest John's office at Tammany Hall and sat down behind the desk."[39] And no one challenged the powerfully built, steel-eyed block of granite behind that desk. Genuflection had ended. The stakes were too high and overwhelming to yield possession to anyone.

With Croker's strong hand now at the helm, a rejuvenated Tammany organization once more became a potent political force in the city. Coupled with incredible mistakes by the rival county Democracy and their disheartening decline, and a consequent weakening of reformism locally, Croker masterminded a Tammany triumph in the election of City Chamberlain Hugh J. Grant as mayor in 1888. In return, Grant appointed his sponsor city chamberlain in April 1889. What Croker knew about finances, trust-fund investment, contracts, budgeting and the like, he knew Tammany-wise. He also became chairman of the Tiger's Finance Committee, which kept no books![40] So effectively and thoroughly did he become a Tammany-style leader and master his job, however, that he became a threat to the Republican party in the state. Inasmuch as he allied Tammany with the Brooklyn Democracy and with Democratic Governor David B. Hill, who was a power upstate—giving the Democratic party in New York State tremendous aggregate strength—he had to be contained and humbled by the opposition. Hence the Fassett Investigation, unleashed in 1890.

IV

The first major assault by Thomas C. ("Boss") Platt and his Republican cohorts upon Croker's newly constructed, machine-crafted citadel came with what was popularly known as the Fassett Investigation. Pursuant to a resolution adopted January 20, 1890, by the state senate, its Committee on Cities was authorized "to pursue certain investigations, with reference to the government of the cities of the State."[41] J. Sloat Fassett (Republican, Elmira) was chairman.[42] His three Republican upstate colleagues were Frank Hendricks (Syracuse), Gilbert Deane (Copake) and Donald McNaughton (Rochester). The three Democrats were Lispenard Stewart and John F. Ahearn of New York, and James Birkett of Brooklyn.

On Fassett's motion, the chairman was authorized to retain as counsel the law firm of Tracy, MacFarland, Ivins, Boardman & Platt.[43] In view of the fact that this was so decidedly a prominent *Republican* law firm, with the Platt being Frank H. Platt, the Boss's son, and another partner being Benjamin F. Tracy, Jr.—then absent in President Benjamin Harrison's cabinet as secretary of the navy—the partisan outlook of the majority of the Fassett Committee was clear. With the possible exception of William M. Ivins, who had been judge advocate general of the state of New York and was to run as the unsuccessful Republican candidate for mayor of New York in 1905, and was to build a wide reputation later as investigative counsel and cross-examiner in official probes, this firm was more to be noted for political muscle than legal acumen. Five hundred subpoenas were to be prepared, an ominous portent for Tammany, especially.[44]

Although the presumed intent was to investigate Brooklyn, Albany, and Troy, as well as New York City, the true target was the last-named city's departments and through them to get at Croker and Tammany.[45] The *New York Times* called it "a big contract for a Senate Committee," yet admitted that the state senators from the other cities singled out had been thrown into consternation. Editorially, however, the *Times* was more cautious and even explained the announced benefits. The resolution was, "ostensibly at least, intended to promote the general cause of reform and improvement in city government." The objective was "to ascertain the faults and defects of municipal administration and the causes of the same, and find out the means of correcting them." On the other hand, there should be protection "from legislative tinkering, and the essential requirement of a thorough reform is absolute control of local authorities over local affairs without interference from State authority."[46] The timeless conflict between state and city, between central authority and local autonomy, between upstate Republicans and downstate Democrats, between a Platt and a Croker.

The Fassett Investigation, however, has a special significance in this essay on Richard Croker. There is a perverse logic to its being made arbitrarily our terminal point. It laid him bare. It is the event that cast ahead the shadow of his leadership. In power but five years in 1890, with over a decade yet to go, he had his motivations revealed, much of his methods, his personality and his character, and his goals. The next two-thirds of his reign were to give him polish and remove much of his crudities, and refine his techniques into more sophisticated patterns. Fassett showed what Croker was bringing the city down to, and what its prospects were at his hands. The testimony by him and about him is an encapsulation of the man—and therefore a case study in machine politics in a booming, sprawling city bursting at the seams. It also carries a lesson as to whether last hurrahs should not be striven after by a concerned citizenry.

When the investigation began on February 20, 1890, Ivins was instructed to prepare a series of questions relative to the manner of appointing and removing heads of municipal departments and bureaus, the method of collecting revenues, assessing taxes, the sources of revenue, the objects of expenditures, bonded indebtedness and the purposes for which incurred, and any other pertinent questions, "and which questions may be addressed by letter to the mayors of the several cities in the State, as the committee may direct."[47] In turn, Ivins disclosed that he had earlier been directed by the committee to prepare a summary of the acts affecting the governments of the several cities for the decade 1880-1890; and, in respect to New York alone, there were 390 such statutes, not counting enabling acts.[48] Hendricks, chairing that first session, announced that the investigation would be conducted "solely in the interest of good government and with no partisan motive whatever. . . . We are not sitting as a court, but . . . conducting a legislative inquest [not the happiest choice of words!] " in order to report back to the Legislature.[49]

Hendricks's reassurance became empty rhetoric when Ivins declared that whereas the mayors of the other cities in mind had been given the same set of forty questions to answer, New York's mayor had a special set directed to his attention.[50] The metropolis was truly the quarry. There may have been justification, but there should have been no illusion. Now that the preliminaries were over, the hunt was on.

Croker, however, was out of reach! In the van of the investigation, he had resigned as city chamberlain on February 8, 1890, ostensibly because of ill health, and had repaired to Europe—especially to Wiesbaden, Germany, one of the continent's great spas. As a result, not surprisingly, the first witness was Mayor Hugh J. Grant, who as an alderman in 1883-84 had been the only untainted Tammany member of the "Boodle" street traction franchise scandals of that time.[51] Ivins introduced Grant's message to the Board of Aldermen for 1889 to show how New York was governed:

Many of the laws . . . have by successive enactments been reduced to a state of confusion which makes their enforcement and even their interpretation, exceedingly difficult while the local ordinances emanating from various departments clothed with the power of enacting them, are seldom understood by the people and often irreconcilable with each other.[52]

Grant now testified that New York should have, like most of the cities in the Union, a municipal code; that some city departments had authority to make their own rules which had the force of law; others had less authority, and there seemed to be confusion and no uniformity. Some ordinances were questionable because of the doctrine of implied repeal. Furthermore, as in the case of the sanitary code, the aldermanic ordinances were in conflict with the code.

In addition, Ivins drew from the mayor the oblique inference that

Tammany, which had drafted and advocated a bill seeking the abolition of the office of chamberlain when Ivins had held that office, had dropped its quest when *Croker* was appointed chamberlain. Moreover, some heads of departments were appointed, some were elected; some were single-headed, others were double-headed.[53] Street railway franchises shortly came up. Fassett himself had introduced a bill for their sale, and Grant too had sought to have one introduced for the same purpose. The differences between their two bills defined Tammany's philosophy. Fassett wanted the sale for a given number of years, to be paid for in cash—dollar for dollar of stock. Grant would have bestowed a franchise in perpetuity, and the operator's stock could be issued *without limitation* to contractors for work done to ten times the fair value of the work. In the projected rapid transit commission, Grant refused to recognize the impropriety of appointing five Tammany Hall commissioners. He could not even remember the provisions of his own bill.[54]

The mayor, questioned about his conduct when sheriff of New York County, testified that he had "made no distinction" between his official moneys and those that came in from his other incomes; that he had mingled these funds, placed them in the bank, and that he deducted as needed from the deposits. He kept no books to record what and when he drew out for shrieval or personal purposes, and admitted to an incredulous Fassett that he "often made payments without making any entries upon books." He did not know whether he had his canceled checks and, when pressed, could not show a record of disbursements or what his cash balance was at the end of the year. Compounding this chaos was the additional disclosure that he kept his moneys in several banks. Furthermore, Grant was unable to show how much money—during his incumbency—from gross proceeds had been expended to pay him, his deputies, and for advertising and expenses. For every fee his deputies earned, he "got half the poundage."[55]

Although the mayor tried to obscure the fact, he apparently extracted a share of his deputies' gratuities if they were large enough to pass by statute as "extra compensation." Ivins cut through his evasions to accuse him of charging double the fees that auctioneers received for sales and foreclosures by assignment, and pocketing half for himself.[56] It was incredible that Grant could compel William P. Kirk, a liquor dealer and a Tammany leader and former alderman, to take in an unwanted partner, one John F. B. Smyth, and not even be given a reason.[57] The distinguished Bourke Cockran, who was present as counsel to Tammany, justified whatever Grant had paid out to others for services performed for him when sheriff, even if the courts had awarded ten times that payment's amount to Grant. "Justify it?" he retorted to Fassett, "I advised it."[58]

Introduced into testimony was a presentment, dated March 25, 1890, from a grand jury of the city and county to the Court of General Sessions that ripped into these practices. Their investigation established that the debtors were not consulted in these settlements, and the judgments were returned against them minus the sum allowed the sheriff by the victorious creditors. "The injustice and injury resulting therefrom are manifest." Actually, where a deputy acted instead of the sheriff, the latter received nine-tenths of the poundage and one-half the auctioneers' commissions. How much more profit than this the sheriff received "can not be ascertained with any accuracy from his books, as no proper record of those receipts has been kept"—indeed, so loosely kept "that very little satisfactory information can be obtained from them." The grand jury's highly critical summary of "the full means and variety of these evils" during the previous three years coincided with Richard Croker's coming to power and his exercise of it. Grant was, in turn, his creature, his protégé.[59]

Other disclosures brought out that saloons close to polling places stayed open illegally on election day; and, that it was fairly clear that franchises and petitions to change street railway motive power from horse to cable had to go through Croker and possibly Grant too.[60] Shortly afterwards, it was sheer effrontery for the sardonic Bourke Cockran, on the stand, to answer Ivins's question as to whether Grant and Croker as members of the sinking fund commission were not "very influential and important leaders in Tammany Hall" with this sneering rejoinder: "Tammany Hall has no leaders; those who are generally supposed to be leaders are really followers, among whom I include myself."[61] Ivins was not to be thwarted by his slick adversary. He soon established that the commission, which really meant Croker and Grant, and refined still further meant only Croker, could and did dictate their wishes to the Board of Aldermen through influence and pressure even if in certain matters they had no legal authority.[62] Basically, Tammany wanted home rule, which in pragmatic terms meant *carte blanche* to run the city. Just as basically, the Republicans were fearful of granting it. This had been the battleground for forty years, and it was to continue for almost another forty years.

Some of the most significant Fassett testimony came from Patrick H. McCann, Croker's brother-in-law. Their wives were sisters, but the two men were estranged inasmuch as Croker's relationship with his wife, Elizabeth, could be said to have cooled. His admissions were damning, but—in fairness to him—he was a reluctant witness. Yet, he warmed to his task and no matter how hard Cockran later attempted to discount and discredit his remarks, Ivins built a case upon them that, with collateral testimony, seemed convincing and could not be shaken.

Essentially, McCann admitted that Croker had come to his store with about $180,000 in cash shortly before December 31, 1884, for the purpose of securing sufficient votes in the Board of Aldermen to get Grant confirmed as commissioner of public works. Croker wanted to know whether McCann knew some people in the neighborhood that he should meet. The money had been raised "by the organization" and Grant had himself thrown in $80,000 of it. Grant never got the nomination, but there was no knowledge of whether the money had ever been returned to the donors.[63]

In reply to Ivins, McCann testified, yes, he had been told by Mrs. Croker that Grant while sheriff had given $25,000 to Croker's daughter Flossie in the form of $5,000 each in envelopes on five separate occasions! Grant was to maintain that it was $10,000, in two $5,000 installments.[64] The gifts "paid for the house they live in" on Mt. Morris Avenue. Moreover, Leicester Holme, (now) Mayor Grant's private secretary, had visited Mrs. Croker often—"three times in one day"—and offered her a sizable sum of money to leave the city during this investigation and go to Germany. Holme had also visited Dr. J. C. Beekman, her family doctor, proposing "to pay his expenses and pay him what his practice would be supposed to pay him during his absence"—obviously so that he would persuade and accompany her.[65] Apparently, Mrs. Croker had declined the offer, and it may have had to do with what Ivins alleged ("Mr. Croker's family relations are unpleasant and unhappy") and McCann consequently was assisting to maintain his sister-in-law's family to the extent of some $4,000. The debt was "continuous," long-standing, and still unpaid, and had arisen from

sending supplies from Mount St. Vincent, paying his bills outside, paying them to-day; he left his finances in such a way that his wife could not get along; I am paying her bills, so that she could keep the few dollars that he left her in such a way that if the worse came to the worse I would stand by her.[66]

The Croker house itself testified to the relationship between Kelly and Croker, and the power of the organization. Kelly had gotten an act passed by the Common Council to construct it in 1883 for the city park commissioners and then arranged to get his protégé a half-interest in it plus its lease. Croker and Kelly apparently expected to lease it out at a profit, but their speculation misfired, and "they lost money."[67]

In the session of May 3, Ivins (who obviously was thoroughly armed with data on Croker), brought forth further information from McCann about his conversation with his brother-in-law. Croker had wanted Grant in as commissioner of public works because there was a manufacturer of cement on the Hudson River, somewhere near Newburgh, who would give a kickback of 10 cents a barrel if his cement were used in the building of the new city aqueduct, and Grant "could get this cement used in the aqueduct and in the department of public works." Grant denied this altogether as well as that he had contributed $80,000 to Croker's $180,000 slush fund.[68] Ivins's interrogation clearly showed that as Kelly had befriended Croker, so Croker in turn had guided Grant. The mayor admitted that Croker in 1884 had "advised me to have nothing to do with [the corrupt "boodle" sale of the Broadway street railway franchise] for they would be caught."[69] Indeed, all the Tammany aldermen had been implicated, had been prosecuted, or fled—all but Grant, who had heeded well—and it had been a debacle for Kelly. How had Croker known? Why had he not stressed the impending disaster to Kelly and saved other Tammany aldermen? Kelly was presumably boss in these years. To our knowledge, although he was already ill, he was still vigorously active at all levels of the political scene. Grover Cleveland could ruefully confirm this in 1884! Yet, there was Croker already behaving like the boss of the Hall himself. Was he usurping the trappings of office? Was Kelly aware that his lieutenant was inching toward generalship, even if slyly? And did Kelly die in 1886 in time to escape the ignominy of a palace revolution? Thus, for example, whereas "Mr. Kelly had requested the appointment of Judge [John] McQuade" as commissioner of public works, Croker had pressed for Grant's nomination. While neither got it, it was a peculiar reflection on Kelly's status.[70]

In a progress summation up to that point (the end of the May 19, 1890, session), Ivins effectively marshalled the four telling points that McCann had made. First, Croker had an interest in a house in the Mt. St. Vincent area, was already enjoying benefits accruing from a lease on it "at a time when Mr. Croker was himself an officer of the government of the city of New York" (obviously illegal), and had put out so little of his own funds for the property that his partner in the venture, Cornelius S. Conkling, had had to protect himself by arranging for a chattel mortgage on themselves jointly, to be held by McCann. Second, Croker had brought the $180,000 designed to bribe aldermen into McCann's presence, and the latter had arranged for him to meet with a Thomas D. Adams, who might be of assistance in making contacts. Third, Holme had approached Mrs. Croker and Dr. Beekman in an effort to undermine the investigation by having them depart the country. Fourth, Grant had given to little two-year old Flossie Croker for her birthday $10,000 (according to his own account) or $25,000 (by McCann's account), and Croker, in newspaper interviews from abroad, had deprecated the sum "as so insignificant that he does not remember what it was or what was done with it."[71]

It had become ever more clear that Richard Croker's testimony was absolutely essential if the truth were to be gotten, and that he must appear.

V

On Monday, June 23, 1890, Richard Croker was called as a witness and was duly sworn. The courtroom was jammed. He had returned from Germany "to meet those charges that have been made against me." Joseph H. Choate, one of the great deans of the American bar, as his personal counsel, led him through a description of his official career and then quickly into the McCann testimony of the money Croker had shown him for the confirmation of Grant. Croker declared: "It is absolutely untrue . . . in all particulars." He went into a tortuous, labored account of how instead it had been McCann who had invited him to the former's shop to meet Adams, whom McCann was thinking of taking in as a partner. In the conversation between the brothers-in-law, in the Croker version, the Boss testified that there was a rumor all about town that $80,000 had been raised to confirm Hubert O. Thompson, the county Democracy incumbent commissioner of public works, and keep him in office. Croker thought Adams might have some knowledge of it. In addition, McCann wanted his brother-in-law's opinion of Adams as a prospective partner.[72] Croker averred that the gifts to Flossie were two $5,000 sums, not $25,000. As testimony, on and on, it read lame, contrived, and coached.

With Choate still taking him by the hand, Croker testified that his wife and he had taken Grant's $10,000 gift money and invested it in property costing $36,000 at West 147th Street and Seventh Avenue, after adding $6,500 in cash of their own; a bond and mortgage of $20,000 was still outstanding. The purchase had been effected by Mrs. Croker's mother, Catherine Frazier, from Cyrus Field on November 20, 1887. On top of that, Croker, a man who had been in financial straits only a half-dozen years earlier, had been able to purchase additional property in the heart of booming Harlem, at 38 West 125th Street—also through an intermediary, James Keating—on May 6, 1889. The property cost $65,000: $5,000 was paid in; Keating got a $25,000 mortgage from the New York Savings Bank; and the balance of $35,000 was paid in cash! Why Keating? Convenience, said Croker. Also, he might secure a better bargain in another name, and he had a neighbor, Hardy, whom he did not want to know about these purchases. Choate glossed over the source of that $35,000.[73]

Croker admitted that he had gotten the lease for the Mt. St. Vincent hotel through Kelly and the park commissioners with no effort on his part and at a time when he held no public office. He denied owing McCann a cent, and swore that he had provided $300 a month for his wife during his absence. Interestingly, he defended his March 20, 1870, oath, in association with his seven aldermanic colleagues, on no confirmation or approval of ordinances without the consent of certain anti-Tweed leaders, as a rebellion against Tweed rather than a violation of his oath of office. But in the total context of Croker's replies, Ivins would declare:

And I propose consequently in asking these questions to direct attention to the fact that to-day we have in control of the government of New York City the fag ends and tailing of the Tammany Hall of Tweed's day.[74]

Ivins was extremely interested in Grant's remarkably munificent gifts to little Flossie, and bored in on that chink. Relentlessly he pursued with Croker the circumstances of the gifts, their precise dates, whether the child "was standing beside [Grant], or between his knees, or alongside of him," whether the gifts were expected or a surprise, and the conversation that arose between Croker and Grant after the gifts. He then asked about the second $5,000 gift and whether Croker had counted it, the form of the bills, whether the money had been put in a house safe or elsewhere in the home for safety (Mrs. Croker had safes, "little safes in drawers and in trunks"). Had his wife told him where she had put the money away? How, as trustee for his daughter, had he invested her money? The beleaguered boss had either forgotten, could not remember, or was painfully vague. It was obvious that Ivins wanted to leapfrog over Flossie's oblivious head to establish that this had been a political payoff by Grant. Croker, with goads sticking out all over him, sometimes retorted with asperity, but kept just enough wit about him to sidestep the land mines.[75]

What Ivins was also establishing obliquely was that Tammany Hall was decidedly good to its leader. Croker—a man so recently impecunious—admitted that he had kept sums as large as $25,000 or $30,000 in his home.[76] But had Grant's envelopes really been used for investment in realty for Flossie? Ivins suddenly veered to a $100,000 slush fund that it had been rumored was raised in Tammany to .defeat Thompson's reelection by bribing aldermen not to confirm him, thereby throwing the election to another. It was not hard to infer from Croker's testimony that the other was, obviously Grant.[77] Ivins had done a capital job in backing Croker as well as Grant into sufficient corners to strip bare the Boss's goals and tactics.

When Elizabeth Croker came to the stand, she stated that she had been married in 1873. There had been nine children; six still survived. But right down the line she gave the lie to McCann's testimony and corroborated every one of her husband's statements. In her position, could she do otherwise? Remarkably articulate but possibly not quite credible, she declared for example that Leicester Holme had come to her home only to volunteer to get her tickets and a stateroom just as he had gotten Croker's.[78] "There was not much vindication," maintained the *New York Times* editorially,[79] "of Croker and Grant in the testimony of Mr. and Mrs. Croker."

After the Crokers had been excused, and sessions resumed on Monday, October 6, 1890, the investigation turned its attention again to the municipal departments. The Board of Excise, examined into, was accused of fraud, hardly cracking down on offenders, and of winking at relicensing their premises under new names. The board was also castigated by the *Times* as inefficient, and its methods lax. In passing, it was noted that the state Civil Service Commission was just about useless in those procedures that related to the excise functions.[80] When Tammany won the mayoral election in 1888, there had been a wholesale patronage housecleaning of incumbents, with at least two-thirds of the employees in the Board of Excise having been changed within a few months. When the Tammany workers and supporters marched in, the county Democracy heads were the first to roll. Stephen O'Brien, brother of the hated former sheriff and an inspector, was the very first casualty. Tammany district leaders made recommendations which were tantamount to decree (George Washington

Plunkitt, state senator and leader of the Seventeenth Assembly district, Judge John McQuade, heading the Twenty-second, and Police Commissioner James J. Martin, were among the examples cited). When prominent Republican Hamilton Fish, Jr., requested the appointment of one James Delaney, the appointment was made after President of the Board Edward T. Fitzpatrick "found out that Mr. Delaney was acceptable." Ivins pressed:

> Q. Acceptable to whom?   A. The organization.
> Q. What organization?   A. Tammany Hall.

This was a devious admission by Fitzpatrick that it had to be cleared with Richard Croker.

Had the Boss himself taken advantage of the verdant opportunity? At least to the extent of recommending the appointments of the secretary, chief clerk, and cashier, if not untold others. Only once was a request of his turned down, and that because Mark Lanigan was in the liquor business, a flagrantly illegal conflict of interest! Out of 135 persons employed in the excise office, only one was a non-Tammanyite.[81] In addition, the implication was strong from the testimony that many of these hacks moonlighted, and tended bars if they did not own them. Also running through the cross-examinations was a strong skein of evidence that competency, qualifications, experience, and the previous employment of candidates or applicants were hardly, if ever, checked out.[82] It was apparent that Tammany Hall and the liquor trade enjoyed a powerful mutual attraction and that the organization had no intention of quarreling with the saloon. In the public mind, this association was to become an indelible affinity.

By an interesting coincidence in timing, the Tammany Committee of Twenty-four met on October 6 to select their municipal slate of candidates. This committee was the power center of the party, dominated by Croker and his personal coterie—Grant, Cockran, and Thomas F. Gilroy (who would succeed Grant as mayor)—and no nominations or policy decisions would take place without an order from Croker. "Tammany Hall was never so close a corporation as it is to-day, and that means that the City Government was never manipulated to so great an extent by so few men as it is now."[83]

VI

The Senate Committee on Cities reported back to the state senate on April 15, 1891.[84] The 135-page report was less partisan than Tammany might have had cause to fear, especially in view of the spirited grilling of its chief and the general embarrassment it suffered from the testimony. Croker was hit *en passant* but not conspicuously by name. Perhaps its major conclusion came close to the beginning. "Under the existing system," Fassett and his colleagues declared,

stability of city government is a practical impossibility. The officers of our municipalities find it impossible to determine upon any general policy whatever looking towards better administration with the expectation that any such policy can ever be carried out to its proper and logical conclusion. This is due not only to the continued possibility of legislative interference, but because of the pertinacity with which interested parties or local authorities appeal to the [State] Legislature year after year in matters affecting city government—from the most important to the most insignificant—thus depriving the cities of their administrative autonomy, and subjecting them to conditions which do not prevail in the administration of the business of any other corporation whatever.[85]

The people themselves were blamed largely for indifference to their local authorities' policies and for failing to protect both themselves and the state legislature by knowing and disclosing the facts. All these conditions "produce waste and mismanagement" that would not exist in a private corporation. Moreover, it was "frequently impossible for the Legislature, the municipal officers, or even the courts to tell what the laws mean." Municipal government as then constituted was "a mystery even to the experienced." Municipal officers were not even certain of their tenure.

It may give a student of city government a curious, uneasy sensation, a feeling of *déjà vu*—in light of New York City's present staggering problems—to consider the following indictment:

That local authorities receive permission to increase the municipal debt for the performance of public works which should be paid for out of taxes. That the conflict of authority is sometimes so great as to result in a complete or partial paralysis of the service. That our cities have no real local autonomy. That local self-government is a misnomer; and that consequently so little interest is felt in matters of local business that in almost every city in the state it has fallen into the hands of professional politicians.[86]

There was a pervasive appeal for home rule, even to the point of recommending an amendment to the state constitution to achieve a greater degree of it and prevent "charter tinkering." But so had *Tweed* pressed for home rule! With more experience drawn from history, the committee might better have urged the thorough laying of the groundwork for educating the citizenry and reform before advocating the seeding.

Certain of the individual municipal departments were gone into and their operations (and inadequacies) analyzed.[87] In the area of taxation, expenditures, and indebtedness, for example, it was recommended that the comptroller file annual financial reports with the state comptroller. It is incomprehensible that this was not already required, but state tax laws would have to be radically amended to overcome the local deficiencies and permit the suggested changes for the better. Other findings were summarized. Unfortunately, the police department—among some others—had not been investigated, for this was the department traditionally associated with Croker's name as having been corrupted so seriously as to create a wide-open town by officially winking at prostitution, gambling, and rampant graft. The committee conceded that the situation could not "be thoroughly and completely investigated in a single year, and is a task which requires for the proper execution the greatest skill, experience and patience." In an assessment as true then as it is today, the committee further declared, "In our judgment it is impossible to over-estimate the importance of the problem of municipal government," and followed it with their conclusion:

It is our duty, however, to make the law such that whoever may be the parties or individuals responsible for the government of the city, they shall find absolutely no excuse for bad management in the condition of the laws. But so long as the laws are unintelligible and incoherent these great corporations [incorporated cities] must continue to be mismanaged, and the first and exclusive duty of the Legislature in respect of this is to reduce the laws to a coherent and intelligible whole, and in such a way as to leave as much independence to localities themselves in the administration of their affairs as is possible.[88]

In almost all cases, the recommendations were whistlings in the wind or were many years away, and the city was ordained to reap many whirlwinds as a result. While it is true that the function of the Fassett Committee was purely investigative, their report leaves at least a little pang of regret, if not wonderment, that for all the effort and time expended it did not deal sharply with Croker and on the evidence produced recommend to the legislature some form of punitive action. The threat had passed, and the Crokers of the state could smirk while continuing their predatory ways.

VII

On Sunday, October 5, 1890, while the Fassett Investigation was still in progress, the Reverend Thomas Dixon addressed an audience of nearly twelve hundred persons in Association Hall, Twenty-third Street and Fourth Avenue, calling Croker "our uncrowned king—the silent sovereign of the city." New York City bore the shame of this by tamely accepting his dictatorial rule. "Oh, Lord," Dixon intoned, "how long? how long?"[89]

And the Lord answered, "Until 1902"! In that year Richard Croker's hegemony finally came to an end. In the intervening years he had suffered some setbacks but had mainly garnered triumphs, insuring the loyalty of those who fed at the trough until the end approached. He had weathered two further Platt-inspired probes, the so-called Lexow (1894–95) and Mazet (1899) investigations, rubber-stamped by pliant Republican legislators yet of great value in providing us with evidence and knowledge. All in all, Croker's reign, from the points of view of Tammany and machine politics, was highly successful, a masterpiece of careful planning and ruthless execution.

We can understand better the nature and politics of Tammany Hall if we seek out Croker's policies, techniques, and objectives (some already discernible above) that propelled him into power and kept him there until he was eased out as a liability. His method of operation consisted of the following. He maintained iron discipline and inspired fear among his legions, at all levels, producing a paradoxical loyalty. He was a determined bloodhound after patronage, the lifeblood of any political machine. He was a beneficent padrone to those in need of aid or favors, as described by George Washington Plunkitt—a silken chain binding the needy and powerless to Tammany. He completely dominated the Board of Aldermen, the Police Department, and all the municipal services. As a purveyor and practitioner of "honest" and "dishonest" graft alike he made corruption an acceptable (but not respectable!) symbol of political success. He was a master of political bargaining, making easy alliances with men like David B. Hill and pragmatic agreements with men like Thomas C.

Platt. He was astute enough to realize the growing dominance of big business in our economic life during the years of his own ascendancy and the power of its nascent major manifestation, the giant corporation—allying with it and deriving power through franchises and contracts, rewarding or favoring those who cooperated, and punishing those in the enemy camp (bankrupting, for example, the Third Avenue Railway Company, whose management was oriented toward the Republican party). Finally, he drove hard and mercilessly to extend his control over the state as well as the city. These were the complex ambitions and inner drives that made him a veritable powerhouse in the political arena, a fearful adversary, an authoritarian boss.

The Fassett Investigation provided the first real public opportunity to observe and analyze Richard Croker as boss clinically, and to forecast much of his future career and mode of operation. It was not the happiest of revelations for New York City. It was a classic textbook lesson for a city that would not read. Or heed.

NOTES

*   The writer desires to express his thanks and indebtedness to the State University of New York Research Foundation for their grant that permitted him to undertake additional research into the career, objectives, and methods of Richard Croker.

This preliminary essay on Croker, through the time of the Fassett Investigation launched in 1890 to embarrass him politically and weaken Tammany Hall, is to be followed by a full biography at some later date. Considerations of space and arbitrary selectivity have of necessity molded the shape and character of this paper.

Despite, however, the constraints of brevity and modest depth, the writer was happy to accept the invitation of the editor out of affection and respect for Sidney I. Pomerantz. Sidney and he had known each other for some 45 years, as sometime colleagues at City College of New York, as scholars mutually interested in New York politics and affairs, and always as good friends.

The writer hopes that this paper will, even if only in some small measure, testify to his esteem for Professor Pomerantz's outstanding qualities that gave the overworked expression "a scholar and a gentleman" genuine substance and meaning. Sidney was compassionate, deeply concerned for, and devoted to, his students, his college, his colleagues. He was an outstanding teacher, an exceptional researcher, and a man of remarkable catholicity of historical subject matter and encyclopedic information. He deserves to be remembered long and well.

1. *Wall Street Journal*, May 20, 1975.
2. When Mayor Daley died in December 1976, the jockeying and infighting for succession amply demonstrated that political bossism had lost none of its attractiveness. In ethnic and racial enclaves, however, it could be the *first* hurrah. Thus, Alderman Michael A. Bilandic, a Croatian, became Chicago's acting mayor, while the black community was disappointed that its own William Frost (next in line to Daley) was bypassed and shunted into the chairmanship of the aldermanic committee vacated by Bilandic.
3. The writer is greatly indebted to his colleague Dr. Arthur L. Galub, professor of political science at Bronx Community College, for many illuminating insights and an analysis of the political theory in this moot area. In this connection—now fashionably termed "executive-centered coalition"—others than mayors alone should be cited. One may turn to a state assemblyman like Joseph M. Margiotta of Nassau County, a borough président like Manhattan's Percy E. Sutton, or City Councilman Samuel D. Wright of Brooklyn, or a county executive like Nassau's Ralph G. Caso, or state leaders like Joseph F. Crangle, Patrick J. Cunningham, and Richard M. Rosenbaum, in New York. Nelson A. Rockefeller and the late Thomas E. Dewey were historic examples of the political power that governors could possess and exercise. Nor can Alex Rose, the "Gentle (Labor Union) Boss," who also passed away in December 1976, be overlooked or omitted from the machine roster. It has surely been noted that in even this miniscule sampling party affiliation was not mentioned. The struggle for power is not confined to any one party or political creed. No weapon ever is.
   A useful and suggestive bibliography might include the following works: Robert A. Dahl, *Who Governs?* (1961), dealing originally with the concept of the "executive-centered coalition"; Edward C. Banfield and James Q. Wilson, *City Politics* (1963); Edward C. Banfield (ed.), *Urban Government* (1969); Harold F. Gosnell, *Machine Politics: Chicago Model* (1969); Eugene Lewis, *The Urban Political System* (1973); Leonard I. Ruchelman (ed.), *Big City Mayors: The Crisis in Urban Politics* (1969); Francis J. Sorauf, *Party Politics in America* (1972); and Murray S. Stedman, Jr., *Urban Politics* (1972).
4. Mayor Daley, for example, enjoyed additional political clout by virtue of also having been chairman of the Cook County Democratic Central Committee.
5. Lyle W. Dorsett, "Bosses and Machines in Urban America," in *Forums in History*, FA 029 (1974), passim.
6. See, for example, Harvey C. Mansfield, Jr., "Hobbes and the Science of Indirect Government," a superb and erudite analysis, in *The American Political Science Review*, 65 (March 1971): 97–110.
7. Henry Champernowne [pseud. for David MacGregor Means], *The Boss: An Essay upon the Art of Governing American Cities* (New York, 1894), pp. 8, 9.
8. There is no scholarly, full-length biography of Richard Croker. An account of his life and times has to reduce itself to a mosaic whose bits are compounded from those items that are safe to extract from such biographical sources as do exist, occasional letters, primary sources as they are stumbled upon, official documents and investigations, cross-references in other biographies, accounts and commentaries, and much luck.
   The major biography of Croker is Lothrop Stoddard's *Master of Manhattan: The Life of Richard Croker* (New York, 1931), with little scholarship to recommend it. See also Alfred Henry Lewis, *Richard Croker* (New York, 1901). *The Boss, and How He Came to Rule New York* (New York, 1903), by the same author, is a thinly disguised fictional biography of Croker. For briefer accounts, see William B. Shaw, "Richard Croker," *Dictionary of American Biography*, 4:558, 559 (especially the bibliography); Alfred Connable and Edward Silberfarb, *Tigers of Tammany: Nine Men Who Ran New York* (New York, 1970), chapter 7, passim; Harold Zink, *City Bosses in the United States:*

A *Study of Twenty Municipal Bosses* (Durham, N.C., 1930), chapter 5, passim; *New York Evening Post, The "New Tammany": Interesting Biographical Sketches of Its Leaders* (New York, 1890?), section on "The Big Four," pp. 5, 6; *Tammany Times, 4th of July Souvenir* (New York, 1894), pp. 38, 39; Rhadamanthus [pseud. for C. Ammi Brown '97 and Goldthwaite H. Dorr '97], *A History of Tammany Hall* (awarded a Bowdoin Prize by Harvard College in 1896; privately published in New York in 1955), chapters 7 and 8, passim; *Tammany Leaders and Favorites* (n.d., in Yale Univ. Library), pp. 5, 6; Allan Franklin *The Trail of the Tiger* (New York, 1928), pp. 161–272, passim; John D. Townsend, *New York in Bondage* (New York, 1901), chapter 24, passim. There are also histories of Tammany Hall by Morris R. Werner (1928) and Gustavus Myers (reissue, 1971).

9. Stoddard, pp. 1–3, 14–20; Zink, pp. 128, 129; Lewis, p. 13; Shaw, p. 558; Connable and Silberfarb, pp. 198, 199.

10. Lewis, pp. 14, 15; Shaw, p. 558; Stoddard, p. 23; Rhadamanthus, p. 57.

11. *Testimony Taken before the Senate Committee on Cities pursuant to Resolution Adopted January 20, 1890.* New York State Senate Document No. 80, 5 vols. Transmitted to the Legislature April 15, 1891 (Albany, 1891), 2:1706, 1707. Croker testifying. Hereinafter cited as Fassett, with volume number.

12. *Tammany Times, 4th of July Souvenir,* p. 38; Zink, pp. 129, 130.

13. The tunnel provided underground access beneath Park Avenue for the Fourth Avenue street railway to Commodore Vanderbilt's New York Central Terminal on Forty-second Street.

14. Franklin, *The Trail of the Tiger,* p. 158.

15. *The "New Tammany,"* pp. 5, 6.

16. *New York Tribune,* Oct. 13, 1868. Cf. Oct. 12 and 14 issues, and John D. Townsend, *New York in Bondage,* p. 158. The *Tribune's* correspondent estimated that "full 5,000 of the most hardened desperadoes of [New York] are now in Philadelphia." The Philadelphia police were well prepared, and the military were near at hand. Nevertheless, more than 10,000 votes were lost to the Republicans through fraud, bogus naturalization papers, and patent violations of the Pennsylvania Registry Act.

17. See Mark D. Hirsch, "More Light on Boss Tweed," *Political Science Quarterly,* vol. 60, no. 2 (June 1945): 269, 270. For a summary account of Richard Croker's career to 1890, see Fassett, 2:1690–92, 1706–23.

18. For greater detail on the Young Democracy and how it turned into a genuine reform party that threatened Tammany's hegemony, see Mark D. Hirsch, *William C. Whitney: Modern Warwick* (New York, 1948), pp. 55–65; and, Hirsch, "Samuel J. Tilden: The Story of a Lost Opportunity," *American Historical Review,* vol. 56, no. 4 (July 1951): 795–99.

19. Cf. *The "New Tammany,"* p. 6; Shaw, p. 558.

20. Townsend, pp. 158, 159.

21. Fassett, 2:1690. Croker testifying.

22. See Shaw, p. 558.

23. Hirsch, "Samuel J. Tilden," loc. cit., pp. 793, 794. Cf. his "More Light on Boss Tweed," pp. 271, 272; and *New York Times,* July 8, 19, 20, 22, and 24, 1871, and sequential issues throughout following weeks. The *Times* had been assailing the Tweed Ring since September 1870, but now it had O'Brien's material as hard, incontrovertible ammunition.

24. Whoever acquired the damaging records, his role became the precedent for the later appointment of reformer–civic leader Andrew H. Green as deputy comptroller on September 16, 1871, under pressure from Samuel J. Tilden and William F. Havemeyer upon the frightened Connolly to ensure safe custody of the vital documents. See "Samuel J. Tilden," p. 794; and, Fassett, 2:1719.

25. *New York Times,* Nov. 6, 1873. Croker received the second-highest vote among the six candidates, 58, 916.

26. *Tammany Times,* op. cit., p. 38. Shaw speaks of fees amounting to $20,000 or $25,000 a year (p. 558), Cf. Howard B. Furer, *William Frederick Havemeyer: A Political Biography* (New York, 1965), p. 172.
27. Furer, pp. 172-75; *New York Times,* Nov. 18–Dec. 1, 1874, passim. Especially valuable was Havemeyer's response to Kelly's suit on November 17.
28. Hirsch, *Whitney,* pp. 82, 83; Allan Nevins, *Abram S. Hewitt, With Some Account of Peter Cooper* (New York, 1935), pp. 295-97; *New York Times, New York Tribune,* Nov. 4–Dec. 14, 1874, passim; Stoddard, pp. 53-56; Townsend, p. 159; Shaw, p. 558; and, *The "New Tammany,"* p. 6.
29. State of New York. *In Senate, Report of the Committee of the Senate of the State of New York, Appointed to Investigate the Several Departments of the Government in the City and County of New York,* March 16, 1876 (Senate Document 79), pp. 56, 58, 228 et. seq. Croker resided at the time at 205 East Thirty-ninth Street.
30. Ibid., pp. 56-61.
31. Ibid., p. 229.
32. Ibid., pp. 59, 229, 243, 244. Elsewhere in the report it was stated that McDonald had served in eighty-nine cases (p. 243).
33. Ibid., p. 60.
34. *New York Times,* Nov. 8, 9, and 22, 1876. The *Times* stated that his Republican opponent, William H. Stiner, would and should be elected (Nov. 6); then reported Stiner as victorious (Nov. 8); next, that Croker had nosed in ahead (Nov. 9). Actually, when the official returns were in on November 21, Croker had 82,398 votes, 3,073 more than Stiner, but the least of the three victorious Democrat candidates (Nov. 22).
35. For an account of the county Democracy, see Hirsch, *William C. Whitney,* pp. 160 et seq.
36. Fassett, 2:1707. Croker testifying.
37. Hirsch, *Whitney,* pp. 188-91.
38. *The "New Tammany,"* p. 6; Fassett, 1:704. Patrick H. McCann and Ivins testifying; Fassett, 2:1691, 1719, and 1720. Croker testifying.
39. Fassett, 2:1718, 1722, and 1751. Croker testifying. Cf. Stoddard, pp. 67-72; Connable and Silberfarb, pp. 202, 203; *New York Times,* June 2, 6, and 9, 1886. Kelly's home was at 34 East Sixty-ninth Street.
40. Shaw, p. 558.
41. *Testimony taken before the Senate Committee on Cities pursuant to Resolution adopted January 20, 1890.* New York State Senate Document No. 80, 5 vols. Transmitted to the Legislature April 15, 1891 (Albany, 1891). As noted, supra, cited as Fassett, with volume number.
42. See Richard B. Morris, "Jacob Sloat Fassett," *Dictionary of American Biography,* 6:296, 297. Basically, however, the chairmanship was rotated at successive sessions.
43. *New York Times,* Jan. 21, 1890.
44. Fassett, 1:4.
45. Four of the five volumes of the investigation's testimony alone dealt with New York City!
46. *New York Times,* Jan. 21, 1890.
47. Fassett, 1:4.
48. Ibid., 1:5.
49. Ibid., 1:8.
50. Ibid., 1:8, 9.
51. See Hirsch, *Whitney,* pp. 210 et seq. Also, *Tammany Times, 4th of July Souvenir,* p. 38; Fassett, 2:1691.
52. Fassett, 1:9.
53. Ibid., 1:10, 11, 14, 15, 48, 51.
54. Ibid., 1:68, 69. Grant testifying.

55. Ibid., 1:101–10, passim.
56. Ibid., 1:144, 145. Cf. auctioneer William A. Topping's testimony, ibid., 1:276, 277.
57. Ibid., 1:306–9.
58. Ibid., 1:361. The even more distinguished Joseph H. Choate was also retained as counsel for the defense by Tammany.
59. Ibid., 1:365–73, passim. Exhibit No. 1.
60. Ibid., 1:423–25. Richard W. G. Welling testifying; and, ibid., 1:516 et seq.
61. Ibid., 1:534, 535.
62. Ibid., 1:535 et seq.
63. Ibid., 1:650–67. McCann testifying. At one point, he slipped and mentioned 1883 as the date Croker had come to see him.
64. Ibid., 1:734–36, 746–50. Grant testifying.
65. Ibid., 1:663–65. McCann testifying. Grant denied he had been behind Holme's visit (p. 736).
66. Ibid., 1:679. McCann testifying.
67. Ibid., 1:671, 672. McCann testifying.
68. Ibid., 1:696–700. McCann testifying; and, ibid., 1:732, 733. Grant testifying.
69. Ibid., 1:707. Grant testifying.
70. Ibid., 1:738. Grant testifying.
71. Ibid., 1:852–55. Ivins recapitulating. Croker had not been in Wiesbaden for three weeks—testifying to his improved health.
72. Ibid., 2:1690–1702. Croker testifying. Cf. *New York Times,* June 24, 1890.
73. Fassett, 2:1702–4. Croker testifying.
74. Ibid., 2:1703–17. Croker testifying; Ivins accusing.
75. Ibid., 2:1723–31. Croker testifying.
76. See Stoddard, pp. 57–60.
77. Fassett, 2:1730–51. Croker testifying.
78. Fassett, 2:1767–71. Elizabeth Croker testifying.
79. *New York Times,* June 24, 1890.
80. Fassett, 2:1788, 1789, 1816, 1817. Cf. 2:1022–25, 1072, 1073, 1210–13; *New York Times,* Oct. 7, 1890.
81. Fassett, 3:1890–95, 2040, 2041. Edward T. Fitzpatrick and Joseph Koch testifying.
82. See Fassett, vol. 3, passim.
83. *New York Times,* Oct. 6, 1890.
84. State of New York. In Senate. *Preliminary Report of the Senate Committee on Cities, Pursuant to Resolution of the Senate, Adopted January 20, 1890,* No. 72, April 15, 1891.
85. Ibid., p. 13. Cf. *New York Times,* April 16, 1891, editorial.
86. *Preliminary Report,* p. 14.
87. Ibid., pp. 20 et seq.
88. Ibid., pp. 134, 135. The report was signed by Francis Hendricks, James W. Birkett, Lispenard Stewart, Gilbert A. Deane, and J. S. Fassett.
89. *New York Times,* Oct. 6, 1890.

1895-A TEST FOR MUNICIPAL NONPARTISANSHIP

Reformers could expect little more than occasional bit parts on the political stage in New York City during the nineteenth century. Machine politicians, generally loyal to the Tammany Hall organization, ran the show much of the time and had nothing but disdain for political understudies who criticized their methods or purposes. Nonetheless, by the last decade of the century public tastes began to change, and the spotlight turned toward the reformers. As a result, these political dissidents were able to mount a serious challenge to the machine, whose limitations were widely publicized at the same time that its excesses began to surpass traditional levels. In 1894 a coalition of reformers, antimachine Democrats, and Republicans turned Tammany out of office and installed its mayoral candidate William Strong at City Hall.[1]

The victorious coalition of 1894 was in many ways reminiscent of those that had challenged Tammany in previous years. It contained the usual hardy band of political professionals seeking new avenues of entry to the spoils of office along with long-suffering Republican loyalists, whose fidelity to party persisted despite years of wandering in New York City's Democratic wilderness. Animating the anti-Tammany vanguard were the reformers, themselves men of differing persuasions. Some were scandalized by the moral laxity of Tammany Hall, others angered by the machine's involvement with corruption and crime. Many were occupied in reducing waste, controlling municipal expenditures, and lowering tax rates, whereas others were committed to a broad range of reforms aimed at improving the lives of New Yorkers. Members of such a disparate band marching under the reform banner might have neutralized, as had often happened in the past, one another and dampened enthusiasm had not a group of younger activists provided the spark and enthusiasm that ultimately carried the anti-Tammany forces to victory. The appearance of this new group, typified by such men as John Jay Chapman, Richard Watson Gilder, R. W. G. Welling, James B. Reynolds, W. Harris Roome, Julius Henry Cohen, and George McAneny, represented a most hopeful development. Rarely had so many young, capable, reform-minded New Yorkers been willing to challenge the machine in open political combat.

The new reformers were not reticent about their motives or uncertain of their objectives. They were committed to attacking a host of municipal problems and responding to an extensive agenda of unmet needs. But nothing could happen, they realized, until the city was freed from the thralldom of partisanship and the particular perversities of Tammany Hall. This would probably require, according to one reform group, a "new American Revolution against the tyrannical government of political parties." There was no reason, reformers contended, why the two major parties should determine the conduct and issues of city politics. Rather, the politics of New York should proceed within a separate sphere, with loose alignments based exclusively upon municipal matters. In such an environment, independent-minded reformers would be in the enviable position of having the political leverage to combat what Richard Watson Gilder decried as "the ineffectiveness of so many good men." And "good men" were what reformers invariably emphasized in their self-portrait. They were, above all, independent, nonpartisan, selfless idealists who would educate the public by setting standards that would elevate the conduct of municipal affairs. They had, however, few illusions about ushering in the millennium. Rather, what was important to them was accepting responsibility and giving battle. To some, the struggle appeared as more significant than the gains that might accrue. Gilder echoed the sentiments of many when he observed that "whether we shall win or not I do not know. I have never concerned myself much about that." Such rationalizations were probably necessary in a struggle where the odds at first seemed so formidable. But in reality there would be no need for excuses, for these doughty reformers were not timid souls easily swept aside. They had thrown down the gauntlet, offered innovative ways of reorganizing the city, and challenged the political bosses to a test of strength at the ballot box.

The anti-Tammany coalition of 1894 had won; but for many of the reformers, the fruits of victory were not very sweet. The new mayor, William Strong, a figure of stolid respectability, was hardly disposed to take up the cudgels in the battle for reform. Nonpartisanship, a principle close to the hearts of most reformers, left him cold or at least confused. He declared publicly his intention to calculate the relative strength of the various political factions that swept him into office and then to apportion city jobs on that basis. Reformers decried this failure to set political organizations aside and to emphasize the competence of particular non-aligned individuals. But then what was to be expected of an anti-Tammany group whose commitment to nonpartisanship was largely rhetorical? For certain reformers the way out of this dilemma was simple: cast off all alliances with traditional partisan organizations and go forth as independents. Present a ticket to the electorate that was not the product of backroom bargaining or the result of factional balancing, but one that exemplified strict nonpartisanship. Only in this way would the true meaning of reform and the possibilities of independent political action be made clear to the people. It would then be up to New Yorkers to vote their approval of or to reject this approach. Within less than a year after the citywide victory of 1894 a group of reformers—despite intense pressures from within their own camp—prepared to put these unconventional ideas to the test.

The election of 1895 should have been uneventful. Rarely did elections for the judiciary and county positions elicit much enthusiasm. The anti-Tammany victory in 1894, however, upset the normal political pattern; therefore, the off-year elections assumed uncommon importance. The result might serve as a barometer of the public attitude toward the changed situation. It would, if certain reformers had their own way, also measure the appeal of nonpartisanship and independency.

Each political organization consulted and defined its own interests as it prepared for the election. The regular Republican organization, overlooked by the Strong administration in patronage matters, planned to run its own candidates independently. Indecision reigned within the reform camp. The more youthful, aggressive members were, as we have seen, deeply disillusioned with Strong's concessions to the political factions. True nonpartisanship, they concluded, would emerge only if the reform party, unencumbered by political obligations, gained office. An editorial in the *Good Government Bulletin,* the organ of the Good Government clubs scattered about the city, stated: "The Clubs have now to make a choice. They may vindicate their right to an independent existence or they may take their place in history with the numerous reform organizations which have lived and failed in the city because they chose to play the two inconsistent roles of reformers and opportunists."[2] John Brooks Leavitt added that the "staying power of our movement is to be tested this year."[3]

The more "conservative" reformers sympathized with the aspirations of the "radical" wing but considered its tactics futile. They displayed no marked enthusiasm for certain of Strong's policies but were anxious to defeat Tammany once more. This would require, they believed, another fusion campaign in which all reformers and Republicans stood together. Tammany, on the other hand, hoped the election would serve as a fore-runner to its return to power. Boss Richard Croker arrived from England on September 20, 1895; as usual, he announced his permanent retirement from politics.[4] Soon afterward, the Tammany campaign under his direction got under way.

Elements within the Good Government clubs, wherein lodged the advanced reform spirit, moved early in the hope of gaining a tactical advantage. They announced their intention of placing an independent ticket in the field.*[5] Immediately voices cautioned against precipitous action and for delay until the political situation assumed sharper definition. At the annual Good Government convention, members leaning toward fusion advised those disposed toward an independent campaign against nominating a ticket of their own. Joseph Larocque, a former member of the Committee of Seventy, which had orchestrated the anti-Tammany coalition the year before, called upon the independents to remain in the fold and to fight Tammany, as in 1894.[6] The independents, however, repeated their commitment to a strict policy of nonalliance. Joining with the regular Republican organization made them just as uncomfortable as contemplating the return of Tammany. The independent delegation, far more vocal and vociferous than those representing other shades of opinion, gained wide support at the convention and an independent party seemed imminent. Given this likelihood, Republican members of the Good Government clubs drew away and conferred with the Bar Association regarding a possible alternate slate of candidates. The Republican organization meanwhile announced that it intended to prepare a straight party ticket.[7] Theodore

---

*Despite this independent attitude, they were willing to accept judicial candidates proposed by the New York Bar Association.

Roosevelt, a proponent of fusion, deplored the fact that the independents were playing right into the hands of the regular Republicans: "The Republican machine men have been loudly demanding a straight ticket; and those prize idiots, the goo-goos, have played into their hands by capering off and nominating an independent ticket . . . the cowardice and rascality of the machine Republicans and the flaming idiocy of the 'better element' have been comic and also disheartening."[8] Nevertheless, by the end of September, hopes for a fusion ticket grew. The Reverend Mr. Parkhurst, whose blasts against Tammany's immorality had paved the way for victory in 1894, and C. S. Smith, representing the Chamber of Commerce, could report progress in fashioning such an alliance. Conferring with anti-organization Republicans, Good Government men, the state Democracy, and those German-Americans who had not defected to Tammany, they gained adherents for another anti-Tammany front.[9]

The proponents of fusion still faced stubborn resistance from within the anti-Tammany camp. The independents, unmoved by the fusionists' persuasion, concluded that "it was certainly time for citizens to take matters into their own hands and teach the politicians a lesson they will not forget."[10] On September 20, the city convention of the confederated Good Government clubs convened for a long and stormy session. After heated debate, the convention rejected the majority report of the executive committee, which supported fusion. By a vote of 79 to 44, it decided in favor of nominating an independent ticket and eliminated the possibility of a complete fusion campaign—but not entirely.[11] The independents left the door open. They deliberately kept several places on their ticket vacant in the hope that this gesture might attract other parties and thereby confirm their leadership in the campaign against Tammany.

Fusionists believed the independents guilty of serious misjudgment but nevertheless remained hopeful. C. S. Smith considered the independent policy "pitiable." Mayor Strong agreed, and the New York Tribune referred to it as "a mistake of youth, inexperience and impatience." While admitting the sincerity and earnestness of the independents, the fusionists dismissed them as politically inept. Chauncey Depew, a leading Republican spokesman in New York, thought the independents' actions had been premature and ill-advised; he delivered a shrewd analysis of their mistakes. To his mind, the effectiveness of independent action lay in its service as "threatening swords over the heads of crafty politicians." This entailed waiting for the nomination of two tickets and then endorsing the better, or selectively supporting superior candidates from both slates. He considered an independent citizens' ticket a feasible and desirable policy only if both slates were objectionable. Premature action by the independents had placed them in a position where they had to stand up and be counted. Depew thought this unfortunate and unnecessary. It reduced the effectiveness of the movement, whose strength lay in the indeterminate nature of its support. By jumping in first, he felt independents no longer menaced the regular organizations. No longer a nucleus, they became a group distinct and definable. Depew appealed to the independents to withdraw their ticket.[12]

Independents agreed with Depew on their role in the political process but considered the strategy of early nominations as especially effective as a means of exerting influence over the regular party selections. Placing exemplary candidates in the field early, they explained, forced the regular parties to endorse them or to select men of comparable stature. The torrent of criticism, however, did cause some misgivings within the ranks of the independents. There was even some indication that they might yet consent to withdraw their ticket in favor of suitable fusion candidates.

The advocates of fusion, heartened by this possibility, intensified their efforts. As in 1894, the Chamber of Commerce provided the leadership that led to the formation of the fusion ticket. It organized a Committee of Fifty, which contained the eminent and respectable men of the community. This committee contacted the Republican party which, revising its previous position, now accepted the idea of fusion.[13] The Republicans, as a gesture toward fusion, set aside three positions on their ten-man ticket for anti-Tammany Democrats. The New York State Democracy and the German-American Reform Union then joined with the Republican organization and the Committee of Fifty to endorse a ticket of seven Republicans and three state Democrats. Two of the ten, Meyer Isaacs, candidate for the state Supreme Court, and P. Allison, nominated for General Sessions judge, were Good Government men who had already obtained the independent nomination. In a move to enhance its reform image, fusionists drew up the ticket at the City Club. The slate pleased Edward Lauterbach, the Republican city leader, while Mayor Strong declared: "It's a grand good ticket."[14] Cornelius Bliss, a Committee of Fifty member, considered the fusion candidates "good from top to bottom."[15] The *Nation* commended the work of the Committee of Fifty in carrying forward the pattern of reform:

We look on this as an educational agency of the highest value and we are confident that it will be repeated every year until we have created a genuine municipal party strong enough to meet the organization in a fair trial of strength. . . . This continued appearance of nonpartisans successfully parlaying with the party spoilers is to the masses a practical illustration of the nature of the nonpartisan idea.[16]

The independents, though they added two of the nominees to their own ticket, did not abandon it, despite the fact that it now contained four candidates in common with the fusionists. A number of individual Good Government clubs took issue with this decision and defected from the independent camp. The remaining clubs, however, were determined to keep their ticket in the field. Speaking for them, Preble Tucker declared that "if our principles are wrong, let us break up our clubs. If they are not, let us stand firm. We can't afford to support a mere anti-Tammany ticket."[17] R. F. Cutting, James Pryor, and Arthur Von Briesen charged that the fusion ticket departed from the principle of nonpartisanship. They were undoubtedly displeased with New York Republican leader Lauterbach's expressions of satisfaction and the fact that the fusion platform included references to national issues, including an antisilver and a tariff plank.

Responding to the criticisms of the independents, representatives of fusion admitted that their ticket was less than ideal but considered it superior to a straight Republican one. The Committee of Fifty apologetically declared that its candidates "will give a better performance than any other ticket which is now before the people and which has the slightest chance of polling a plurality of votes."[18] J. Harsen Rhoades, a member of the Committee of Seventy in the campaign of 1894 and a Good Government club man who had defected to fusion, thought that the candidates were the best procurable under the situation. Theodore Roosevelt supplied the final justification: "I have had too much experience in politics . . . to refuse to take the best course which is possible at the moment merely because it is not as good a course as it ought to be."[19]

The fusionist profile differed from that of the independents. The campaign leaders of the independents, Preble Tucker, J. Noble Hayes, Alfred Bishop Mason, James Pryor, Boudinot Keith, R. W. G. Welling, John J. Chapman, Arthur Von Briesen, J. B. Leavitt, William J. Schieffelin, R. F. Cutting, John E. Pine, J. H. C. Nevius, Gifford Pinchot, W. Harris Roome, and P. T. Sherman were almost all young men, whereas the Committee of

Fifty's leadership consisted of established businessmen and lawyers of the community. Its finance committee, for example, included J. P. Morgan, Cornelius Vanderbilt, W. E. Dodge, and James Speyer. With the Chamber of Commerce supporting the fusion ticket, financial problems beset the independent movement. Lacking sufficient resources, it nevertheless could count upon enthusiastic and dedicated adherents. The young independents prepared to campaign actively and looked forward to the fight. Chapman wrote to Welling, "Put me down as a speaker every evening—trucks preferred."[20] Reveling in the publicity they obtained, the independents relished the fuss they had stirred up.

The irony of 1895 lay in the fact that the two groups opposed to Tammany spent the entire campaign assailing one another and virtually ignoring their major antagonist. Chapman remarked that "the fusion men have almost stopped fighting Tammany Hall to fight us."[21] The independents hurled charge after charge impugning the motives of the Committee of Fifty. To the independents, the issue appeared clearly drawn. The opportunity for permanent good government, they asserted, arose not from candidates nominated by the machines in the interests of national parties, but occurred when citizens joined together and selected men for office. They inveighed against "the tyrannical government of political parties."[22] An editorial in the *Good Government Bulletin* noted that "the list of the Committee of Fifty contains many of the greatest names in New York, the fusion ticket some of the smallest. Not even its distinguished parentage could confer distinction on such a scrawny babe."[23] The supporters of fusion accused the independents of establishing a "machine" and of adhering to partisan concerns themselves. Gilder attacked the very ground of principle on which the independents stood:

I claim that it is not a matter of principle but of expediency and there is just as high principle in refusing to be led in the line of inexpediency as there is in being led therein. I can imagine a time when all or most of these moral forces would convince each other that it was right to go it alone. If such a time comes I certainly shall throw in everything that I can give to the cause, even if it means defeat, but until that time arrives, I am against such action.[24]

Roosevelt wrote, "It is hard to control my indignation at the action of the goo-goos at running a ticket of their own on grounds that are so trivial that it is very difficult to state them. As for understanding them, why the goo-goos themselves don't do that."[25] Roosevelt also attacked the independents' invocation of a higher principle. He wrote Preble Tucker that "the Good Government ticket falls far short of your ideal. You have carefully striven to maintain a balance between the two parties. The fusion ticket comes quite as near the principles for which you contend as did the ticket which you supported last year."[26]

The burden of the fusion attack, however, was the practical matter of defeating Tammany. An editorial in *Harper's Weekly* criticized the "youthful reformers [who] have not learned the virtue of making haste slowly."[27] They could not expect to change people, it thought, who had voted either Republican or Democrat all their lives. "Ethics must be laid aside and practical politics pursued."[28] Many of the fusionists conceded the sincerity of their independent brethren. Gilder admitted to J. H. C. Nevius that he thoroughly believed in "the perfect sincerity and conscientiousness of yourself and some of your associates and I honor you for your patriotism and it pains me not to be altogether with you."[29] He considered the independent course futile, however, whereas fusion chances were bright.

J. Kennedy Tod lectured Chapman: "For goodness sake, remember that our discussion should not be academic. It is a condition not a theory which confronts us."[30] Fusionist pleas for reason and practicality fell on deaf ears. Even William J. Schieffelin's observation that "should both the fusion and the Good Government tickets be defeated, it will cause a prejudice against our Good Government organization which will greatly weaken it" did not dissuade the independents.[31] Convinced that their mission was of a higher order, they were not interested in practical concerns or in immediate victory. Their campaign was the logical outcome of years of academic discussion of nonpartisanship and the failure to translate it into political terms. Youthful reformers thought it was time to advance beyond the discussion stage and demonstrate to New Yorkers that a political party could eschew partisan considerations. They imagined that their failure to stand on principle would discredit the entire reform movement. Chapman remarked, "The thing that drives us to this course is the impossibility of ever keeping the reform elements together if we sell them out year after year."[32]

"I want the public to get used to independent nominations."[33] These words of Chapman reflected the desire of the independents to educate New Yorkers in the new political dispensation. The independents denied that the Committee of Fifty could perform this function. Consisting of the rich, the established, and the respectable, it was rooted to the methods of the past. The independents believed that only they possessed the fortitude and the tenacity to usher in the political millennium. They were willing to absorb years of defeat until their ideas gained strength and acceptability. As the *Good Government Bulletin* phrased it, the independent movement "demonstrated the existence of an organization designed not to win present success as the only thing worth striving for, but to carry on the fight for good city government from year to year and to gain honorable defeat after a good fight rather than from a victory secured by questionable methods."[34] The independents spoke of political radicalism but were content with deliberate speed. They realized their ideas were in advance of the times, and they were willing to wait.

Practically speaking, the independent movement was a political blunder. The fusion ticket that so angered them was creditable and contained four men whom the independents supported. The major grievance of the independents was the formation of the fusion slate—that is, that it resulted from a conference of political parties, not of citizens. Such a fundamentally esoteric and academic issue could not arouse much indignation or result in widespread support. There was little doubt that Tammany, not the Platt organization, constituted the most formidable enemy in New York City. Bossism could not be overthrown in one campaign, and the importance of defeating Tammany once again could not be overestimated. When all was said about the conscience and the idealism of the independents, one must add that much of it may have concealed the embarrassment arising out of the untenable position in which they found themselves. Meyer D. Rothschild declared, "It was a question of self-respect to stand by the ticket already placed in the field by us."[35] Gilder deftly alluded to the fact when he stated, "Those who think sincerely that they are acting ethically are also acting humanly—they got going and couldn't stop."[36]

The campaign itself was anticlimactic. The excise issue—whether saloons should remain closed on Sundays—dominated the discussion. Tammany stressed the matter of personal liberty and acidly noted that the existence of a Committee of Fifty in 1895 indicated that twenty of the earlier Committee of Seventy had already obtained jobs. The independents sent trucks to the East Side with signs declaring "Down with all bosses." They conducted a spirited but ineffectual campaign. The publicity they received derived solely from the criticism that the fusion forces lavished upon them. The fusion party conducted an active campaign, concentrating upon the improvements that had already resulted from the Strong administration. The public response to the fusion campaign was not encouraging.

Chapman, commenting upon the fusion canvass, noted: "They have lots of money and make a good showing by meetings and in the press, but there is no real enthusiasm anywhere."[37] Enthusiasm, where it existed, was directed toward the Tammany ticket. It swept New York City easily with a plurality of forty-two thousand. New Yorkers probably wanted reform, but they enjoyed their liquor more.

The independents drew a little over a thousand votes. This hardly dampened their enthusiasm. Meyer Rothschild, still manifesting the unrealism of the independent campaign, observed: "Although our vote seems small . . . there were some 50,000 voters registered who did not vote. It would not be strange if from 25,000 to 28,000 of these were Good Government Club members or sympathizers."[38] Chapman was exultant: "We are the people—and there are 1,066 of us, 1,066 rock-ribbed crow-footed googoos that cling to their principles. This is an enormous number of such fellows for a city of two million to produce."[39] The independents had enjoyed the campaign. They had been in the political spotlight and delighted in the publicity. Two days after the election, they celebrated with a gay banquet. With their rashness and youthful exuberance, they had fought for a principle few dared to fight for and had experimented with an uncommon but bold strategy for independent action. Looking back years later, some were surprised at their brashness. Reynolds wrote of supporting the independent ticket, which attracted three votes in his assembly district, adding "I learned something from that experience."[40] Chapman recalled his conduct in 1895 and "wasn't interested in justifying it—indeed I couldn't do it again—it was youth—useful youth."[41]

The lesson of 1895 was not forgotten. The independents learned how important it was for the antimachine elements to stick together to assure an effective challenge to Tammany. But while they learned to fit in, they also left their mark. Their actions in 1895 and on other occasions demonstrated that their participation in an anti-Tammany coalition could not be taken for granted. As a result, their ideas for municipal improvements in New York received respectful attention, because politicians now realized that only in this way could they hope to tap the energy and enthusiasm such reformers could bring to the political arena.

NOTES

1. For further information on the political reform scene in New York City, see Robert Muccigrosso, "The City Reform Club: A Study in Late Nineteenth Century Reform," *New York Historical Society Quarterly*, 52 (July 1968); Augustus Cerillo Jr., "The Reform of Municipal Government in New York City: From Seth Low to John Purroy Mitchel," *New York Historical Society Quarterly*, 57 (January 1973); Steven Swett, "The Test of a Reformer: A Study of Seth Low, New York City Mayor, 1902–3," *New York Historical Society Quarterly*, 44 (January 1960); Edwin R. Lewinson, *John Purroy Mitchel: The Boy Mayor of New York* (New York, 1965); Arnold Rosenberg, "The New York Reformers of 1914," *New York History*, 50 (April 1969); Richard Skolnik, "Civic Group Progressivism in New York City," *New York History*, 51 (July 1970); Jeremy Felt, "Vice Reform as a Political Technique: The Committee of Fifteen in New York, 1900–1901," *New York History*, 54 (January 1973).
2. *Good Government Bulletin*, September 21, 1895.
3. Ibid., August 3, 1895.
4. *New York Tribune*, September 21, 1895.
5. *Good Government Bulletin*, July 6, 1895.
6. Ibid., August 31, 1895.
7. *New York Tribune*, September 19, 1895.
8. Theodore Roosevelt to Henry C. Lodge, October 3, 1895, in Elting E. Morison (ed.), *The Letters of Theodore Roosevelt* (8 vols., Cambridge, 1951–54). Cited hereafter as *Roosevelt Letters*.
9. *New York Tribune*, September 27, 1895.
10. *Good Government Bulletin*, September 14, 1895.
11. *New York Tribune*, October 1, 1895.
12. Ibid., October 13, 1895.
13. Ibid., October 4, 1895.
14. Ibid., October 9, 1895.
15. Ibid.
16. *The Nation*, October 10, 1895, p. 250.
17. *New York Tribune*, October 9, 1895.
18. Ibid., October 20, 1895.
19. Theodore Roosevelt to Seth Low, 1895, Low Papers, Columbia University.
20. J. J. Chapman to R. W. G. Welling, October 15, 1895, Welling Add MSS, New York Public Library.
21. J. J. Chapman to Elizabeth Chanler, November, 1895, Chapman Papers, Harvard University.
22. *New York Tribune*, October 19, 1895.
23. *Good Government Bulletin*, October 12, 1895.
24. R. W. Gilder to John Nevius, October 16, 1895, Gilder Papers, New York Public Library.
25. Theodore Roosevelt to Henry C. Lodge, October 20, 1895, *Roosevelt Letters*.
26. Theodore Roosevelt to Preble Tucker, October 22, 1895, *Roosevelt Letters*.
27. *Harper's Weekly*, October 12, 1895, p. 960.
28. Ibid., November 2, 1895, p. 1032.
29. H. W. Gilder to J. H. C. Nevius, October 25, 1895, Gilder Papers.
30. J. Kennedy Tod to J. J. Chapman, October 26, 1895, Chapman Papers.
31. W. J. Schieffelin to J. J. Chapman, October 17, 1895, Chapman Papers.
32. J. J. Chapman to Mrs. Chapman, October 14, 1895, Chapman Papers.
33. Ibid., October 15, 1895.
34. *Good Government Bulletin*, August 21, 1895.
35. Ibid., October 12, 1895.

36. Gilder to Nevius, loc. cit.
37. J. J. Chapman to Mrs. Chapman, October 30, 1895, Chapman Papers.
38. *New York Tribune*, November 6, 1895.
39. J. J. Chapman to Mrs. Chapman, November 7, 1895, Chapman Papers.
40. J. B. Reynolds to Wheeler Peckham, September 20, 1899, Reynolds Papers (privately held).
41. J. J. Chapman to Mrs. Chapman, December 13, 1897, Chapman Papers.

INDEX